Organic Manual

Organic Manual

Natural Organic Gardening and Living
For Your Family, Plants, and Pets

by

Howard Garrett

TAPESTRY PRESS
WYOMISSING, PENNSYLVANIA

Tapestry Press
1401 Parkside Dr. North
Wyomissing, PA 19610
610-375-1422   www.tapestrypressinc.com

Printed in the U.S.A.
12 11 10 09 08   1 2 3 4 5

Library of Congress Control Number: 2008920892

ISBN 978-1-930819-57-3

Book design and layout by
D. & F. Scott Publishing, Inc.
N. Richland Hills, Texas

For my daughter and radio announcer,

Logan Garrett

Contents

Foreword

Modern communications and the increased speed of travel have virtually turned the whole planet into our visible landscape. There are no new frontiers. Most habitable land is being used and abused with the overuse of chemical fertilizers and toxic pesticides.

Thinking people are quickly realizing the pollution this adds to our already overburdened environment. But, although information on natural organic farming and vegetable gardening is becoming more and more available, the commercial landscape contractor and the urban dweller with the small bit of nature surrounding his home has up until now been mostly forgotten.

Now, with the *Organic Manual,* Howard Garrett has met this need. The *Organic Manual* combines Howard's immense knowledge of and experience in landscape design and installation with his desire to work in harmony with nature. It's a masterpiece for the home and commercial landscaper.

Howard has a great talent for communicating and the courage it takes to tell the truth. His book not only points out the damage some horticultural chemicals do and shows how they lead down a dead-end road, but gives sensible, earth-friendly alternatives that perform as well as and, in the long run, better than toxic chemicals.

Whenever someone speaks out to try to change the current system, he is sure to draw criticism, and I imagine that Howard Garrett has and will draw his share. But, then, how long can the truth be criticized?

> Malcolm Beck
> Organic Farmer
> Founder of Garden-Ville
> Author of *The Garden-Ville Method:*
> *Lessons in Nature, Secret Life of Compost,*
> *Texas Organic Vegetable Gardening, and*
> *Texas Bug Book.*

Acknowledgments

I would like to thank all of the people in the world who have devoted years of their lives to advancing the practice of organics. Among them are Sir Albert Howard, William Albrecht, J. I. and Robert Rodale, T. L. Senn, Charles Walters, Dr. Phil Callahan, Bargyla Rateaver, Arden Anderson, Malcolm Beck, John Dromgoole, Bob Webster and others.

I would also like to thank my family, friends, associates, readers, listeners, and ground crew members who have all helped in their own ways.

Thanks should also go to my clients who have been open-minded enough to allow organic techniques and products to be used on their properties. They include Frito-Lay National Headquarters in Plano, Texas; Sabre Holdings Corporation in Southlake; Carrington Laboratories in Irving and Costa Rica, Fluor Corporation in Irving, Texas Instruments in Richardson, Radio Shack in Fort Worth, Iscar Metals and Tierra Verde Golf Club in Arlington, and many farmers, ranchers and residential friends.

About the Author

Howard Garrett is a 1969 graduate of Texas Tech University, a landscape architect, arborist, publisher, columnist, broadcaster, and organic horticulturist from Pittsburg, Texas. He currently lives in Dallas with his wife Judy. Daughter Logan, at this printing, is a student at U.C. Santa Barbara, in California.

Having started his education in avoiding toxins in 1985 with the birth of Logan, Howard committed his entire career to the research into, education about, and promotion of organic landscaping, gardening, farming, and basic soil management in 1988. He has converted many commercial and residential projects to organic programs.

Thousands of homeowners have now switched to his organic program. Not only are these properties doing well, but they are in better shape than they ever were on synthetic chemical programs. They are also costing less to maintain, and a big part of the savings is a dramatic drop in water use for irrigation.

Howard is host of the KSKY Organic Gardening Radio Show on Saturdays, which is syndicated by Salem Communications across the country on Sundays. He is also a columnist for *The Dallas Morning News* "The Natural Way" in Friday's House and Garden section. He is also host of the world's most used natural organic gardening website—www.DirtDoctor.com. He is the president of the Texas Organic Research Center (TORC).

Howard has written many books including *Plants of the Metroplex, Plants of Houston, Howard Garrett's Texas Organic Gardening, Landscape Design—Texas Style, The Dirt Doctor's Guide to Organic Gardening, Plants for Texas, Texas Organic Vegetable Gardening, Texas Bug Book, Herbs For Texas, and Texas Gardening—The Natural Way*. The vegetable gardening and bug books were coauthored with Malcolm Beck.

INTRODUCTION

Organic Programs are Better in Every Way

Organics is the thoughtful and sensitive use of techniques and products that not only sustain, but improve soil health, plant health, and the environment in general. Synthetic chemical fertilizers and toxic pesticides hurt the soil and plants with every application and are therefore unacceptable.

The practice of growing plants using organic techniques has been used for as long as man has tilled the earth. Only since World War II has the world of agriculture and horticulture been changed by the introduction of toxic synthetic fertilizers and pesticides. The proliferation of these man-made chemicals temporarily increased the yield of many food crops and ornamentals, but it also increased the long-term cost of production, caused pollution of our air and drinking water, changed the soil structure, accelerated erosion, and jarred the entire ecosystem.

Earth's fertile land has been depleted, and overall quality of production has decreased due to a dramatic reduction of the soil's health.

Reasons for the continued use of synthetic products include a lack of understanding of how organic techniques work and the fear that, if chemicals are discontinued, plants won't grow well and will be devoured by insects and disease. The amount of money spent on synthetic chemical advertising and research at major universities is of no small consequence either. Many people simply don't know that organic products work effectively and economically and are easy and fun to use. On the other hand, most folks don't realize how dangerous and damaging harsh pesticides and synthetic fertilizers are, not only to themselves, but to the health of the planet.

TOXIC CHEMICALS VS. ORGANICS

It's not a chemical vs. organics question. Everything in the world is chemical. Even air and water are composed of chemicals such as hydrogen, oxygen, nitrogen, and carbon.

The words "chemical" and "organic" are equally misused and misunderstood. For example, there are products acceptable for use in an organic program that have low toxicity, but are not truly organic; and some organic products are extremely dangerous and not acceptable in a wise organic program.

The point is that the two words, "chemical" and "organic," have become the passwords for the two philosophies. "Chemical" represents the university-taught approach of force-feeding the plants using synthetic fertilizers and trying to control nature using toxic synthetic pesticides, while "organic" represents the approach of working with nature to improve soil health and using only products that increase the chemical, physical, and biological balance in the soil.

It's a big misconception that organic methods are simply safer ways to kill pests. The basis of organics is an overall philosophy of life, not just a simple decision about what kinds of garden or farming products to use. The organic philosophy relates to the ability to see and understand nature's systems and work within those systems. The chemical philosophy teaches that man and his products can control nature. But nature can't be controlled—it's really futile to even try. Many farmers have come to see that and they are now realizing that we must stop taking the carbon and the life out of the soil and the land out of production. The landscaping industry is also moving, although slowly, toward the organic philosophy, primarily because of the tremendous public demand for safer and more environmentally sensitive techniques and products. The biggest surprise is often the fact that organic programs actually save money.

Another difference in philosophy relates to fertilization. Traditional "chemical" proponents say that plants must be fertilized with a 3-1-2 or 4-1-2 ratio fertilizer four times a year. The organic philosophy contends that the soil should be fed and balanced and that plants don't need to be force fed. Balancing the soil is not discussed very often, if ever, in synthetic chemical programs. The synthetic fertilizers are never really balanced. They have a poor compliment of trace minerals and no organic matter or carbon.

The balance of chemistry, physics, and biology is the key. If the soil is biologically healthy, the physics and chemistry will also be in balance. The pH will be between 6.2 and 6.5., earthworms and microbes will be in the proper populations. In healthy soil, calcium will represent approximately 60-70 percent of the available chemical nutrients, magnesium 10-20 percent, potassium 2-5 percent, and sodium .5-3 percent, and all the trace elements should be in their proper relative proportions.

Another advantage of balanced soil chemistry is that fertilizer inputs can be greatly reduced. Once the soil is balanced properly, the maintenance of plants can be done primarily with mulches, compost, foliar feeding, and an occasional application of carbon based natural organic fertilizers.

A chemically, physically and biologically balanced soil will have proper tilth, positive drainage, and the correct populations of living organisms. All you have to do is stop killing the life in the soil with the quick-fix poisons. The end result is healthy plants, animals and people.

REVERSING THE CHEMICAL ADDICTION

There are two major soil pollutants—unbalanced, high-nitrogen, synthetic fertilizers and toxic pesticides. Synthetic fertilizers are the most common chemicals used in farming, gardening, and landscaping. These man-made fertilizers are merely soluble salt compounds, usually found in granulated form, and are relatively inexpensive. Synthetic fertilizers provide nothing to benefit the soil; in fact, they leave considerable amounts of salt residue and other contamination. Their most serious flaw is the lack of carbon.

Since the plants will not absorb large quantities of salt, continued use of salt-based fertilizers can lead to loss of plant quality, loss of productivity, and, in extreme cases, phytotoxicity (poisoning of the plants). These fertilizers repel and kill beneficial soil microorganisms and earthworms, they are harsh and interfere with the natural chemical, physical, and biological systems in the soil, and they feed plants too fast with an incomplete diet.

High levels of nitrates, which are created by synthetic nitrogen fertilizers, are carcinogenic and frequently show up in our drinking water.

Because of the overuse of high nitrogen fertilizers and the plant's inability to use large amounts of nitrogen, the excess is simply leached or washed away and ends up ultimately in our streams, lakes, and aquifers. Some of it volatizes into the air, adding to air pollution.

Pesticides are the second most common chemicals applied to plants and soil. Pesticides include insecticides, fungicides, herbicides, rodenticides and any other poisons used to kill plants or animals. Toxic pesticides disturb or destroy the biological activity of the soil. Pesticides will also affect plant growth, and, when absorbed by the plant, begin passing through the food chain. All living organisms are affected—microorganisms, insects, animals, and people. If used too often at excessive rates, pesticides can virtually sterilize the soil if leaching does not occur—and of course the leaching causes other problems.

When pesticides are leached out of the soil, they end up in streams or ground water, available to enter the food chain again. Huge amounts of toxic chemicals are used on home lawns and agricultural crops, making the use of chemicals a serious problem in urban as well as rural areas. Insects and diseases get blamed for the use of these toxins, but the pests are not the problems, only the symptoms of the problems. The real problem is poor soil health, and that problem is increased with each application of toxic chemicals. Chemical programs create a drug dependency and, unfortunately, they have controlled mainstream agriculture and horticulture since World War II.

The damage to our soil's health can be reversed by returning it to a natural balance. Those of us in the landscape industry and the agriculture industry must take the lead, but homeowners must also get involved in reducing and ultimately eliminating the toxic chemicals we dump into our environment. Besides being dangerous, they aren't necessary. The organic method works better.

Years ago, J. I. and Robert Rodale began the organic movement in the United States using the studies and writings of Sir Albert Howard of England and Dr. William A. Albrecht of the University of Missouri. Rodale convinced many home gardeners and some farmers to add humus to the soil through organic matter and minerals through natural rock powders to improve the health and nutrition of food crops. The idea was quite simple: healthy soil produces healthy plants; healthy plants produce healthy animals and humans. It's possible that the simplicity has been one of the major roadblocks. How could something so simple work? Another powerful obstacle has been the concern, "How are we going to make money?"

The purpose of this book is to explain how the natural organic method works and what products are best to use in a complete organic program. The goal is to convince you to use organic method on the farm, the ranch, in landscaping and in greenhouse operations.

You will learn that organic land management offers reduced long-term costs and liabilities and creates and maintains a safe, healthy environment for all concerned.

Food crops grown organically are a critical ingredient in eliminating disease. The elimination of pesticide residue is important, but not the most important issue. Health is the primary issue, and real health comes from eating food containing a proper balance of mineral nutrients, antioxidants, and energy. Healthy food can only come from healthy soil.

HEALTHY SOILS

S oil and dirt are two very different things. Dirt is an inert planting medium that holds up plants. Soil is a wonderfully dynamic, ever-changing, complex, living system of life, energy, organic matter and minerals. Soil, like all parts of the environment, is fragile. It is also hard to repair once damaged. Unfortunately, most conventional landscape and agriculture procedures have damaged and are continuing to damage the soil. The key is to stop the damage by starting to use management techniques, soil amendments, fertilizers, and pest control products that benefit soil health.

Soil (along with water, air, and sunlight) is one of the basic building blocks of life on earth.

For years the soil has been abused. Taking from the land without giving back to the soil has caused much of the land to become desert, where it was once thriving and productive. Deserts aren't just sand dunes. Dead lakes and rivers are deserts. Chemically abused farms and chemically treated urban lawns are deserts. The definition of "desert" is land that has lost its biological diversity. We can reverse the trend by preserving healthy soil and rebuilding dead and unbalanced soil. We must reestablish biodiversity. A mix of microbes, insects, snakes, frogs, toads, lizards, birds, mammals, annuals, perennials, trees, grasses, herbs, and wildflowers all must be present. Large masses of one plant type or monocultures must be eliminated. Nature abhors straight lines, vacuums, and monocultures. Forests that have been replanted with only one tree species after clear cutting are "deserts." Desertification of the world must be stopped.

Healthy soil is a balance of physics, chemistry, and biology. It is a mixture of minerals, organic matter, living organisms, water, and air. It contains about 25 percent air, 25 percent water, 45 percent minerals, 5 percent humus, and active populations of living organisms. Healthy soil is aerated, rich in organic matter, and alive with insects, earthworms,

Healthy soil is a dynamic living community of air, water, organic matter, minerals, and living organisms.

and microscopic plants and animals. It is well drained, sweet smelling, moist, and rich in a wide variety of minerals and nutrients. It is also highly energized.

ORGANIC MATERIAL AND ORGANIC MATTER

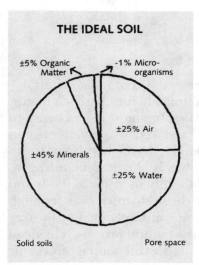

THE IDEAL SOIL

±5% Organic Matter
-1% Micro-organisms
±25% Air
±45% Minerals
±25% Water
Solid soils
Pore space

Organic material is anything that was once living. Every living thing dies, and everything that dies, rots. All organic material biodegrades. It's during that process that microorganisms reduce once-living material into basic elements of fertility.

When organic material such as leaves, twigs, bodies of animals, etc. break down, becoming dark brown and crumbly, the resulting product is organic matter or humus. Humus is soft, crumbly, amorphous, and sweet smelling. It holds and slowly releases water, minerals, and nutrients to the plants. It is the active ingredient of organic material.

Maintaining a constant supply of organic matter is essential to start and continue an organic program. Good sources of organic material to produce organic matter for the soil include composted materials, green cover crops, vegetable and animal waste, root exudates, and the dead bodies of insects and microorganisms.

SOIL MICROORGANISMS

You don't hear much about soil microorganisms from the synthetic chemical horticulturists and farmers. Microorganisms are microscopic plants and animals. They are the "life" in the soil. They include bacteria, fungi, actinomycetes, algae, protozoa, yeast, germs, ground pearls, nematodes, and other microbes. There are about fifty billion microbes in one tablespoon of soil. There are approximately nine hundred billion microorganisms per pound of healthy soil.

To give you a clear idea of the population of these vital microbes, the estimated numbers of common organisms found in each gram of reasonably healthy agricultural soils are roughly as follows:

Bacteria	3,000,000	to	500,000,000
Actinomycetes	1,000,000	"	20,000,000
Fungi	5,000	"	1,000,000
Yeast	1,000	"	1,000,000
Protozoa	1,000	"	500,000
Algae	1,000	"	500,000
Nematodes	10	"	5,000

Note: 1 gram is the approximate weight of a paper clip.

The microorganisms' primary job is to break down organic material—first into humus, then humic acid, and ultimately into basic elements. This process is known as mineralization. Microbes must have a constant supply of organic matter or they will be reduced in population and weaken the soil. Certain microorganisms also have the ability to fix nitrogen from the air, which is approximately 80 percent nitrogen. Unhealthy soil will not support plant growth without artificial foods and stimulants. Healthy soils produce food through microbial feeding. Microbes are constantly being born and are constantly dying. It's okay for microorganisms to die because that is the natural process. The dead bodies of microorganisms are actually an important source of organic matter in healthy soil.

Soil moisture is important to the health of microorganisms. Beneficial microbes thrive in soil that is neither dry nor soggy but about as wet as a squeezed-out sponge. Healthy soil is easier to keep at the proper moisture level and can help to save money on water bills. Biologically active organic soil can save as much as 50 percent of irrigation costs.

Most microorganisms need a constant supply of oxygen. Therefore, aeration of unhealthy soil is critical in the beginning for soil improvement.

ACTINOMYCETES: Actinomycetes generally thrive in well-aerated, neutral to alkaline soils. They are less active in acid or waterlogged soils, but are extremely important to the decay of organic matter in dry regions. They are visible as the white, fungus-like threads on decaying organic matter. The earthy smell of newly plowed soil or the forest floor is compliments of actinomycetes. They are a higher form of bacteria and similar to fungi and molds. Actin-

omycetes are very important in the formulation of humus. Actinomycetes may work near the surface or many feet below the surface. While decomposing animal and vegetable matter, actinomycetes release carbon, nitrogen, and ammonia, making mineral nutrients available for higher plants.

ALGAE: Algae account for the majority of the photosynthetic microflora of the soil. They thrive primarily on or near the soil surface where light and moisture are adequate, although some algae can always be found in the subsoil. Algae produce organic matter by taking carbon dioxide from the air and energy from sunlight to create new cells. They are much less numerous than bacteria, fungi, and actinomycetes, but are extremely important. Blue-green algae (also called cyanobacteria) are able to fix or grab nitrogen directly from the air in the soil.

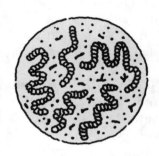

BACTERIA: Soil bacteria thrive under a wide variety of conditions from acid to alkaline and from aerobic (with free oxygen) to anaerobic (lack of free oxygen). Bacteria help in the decay of organic matter, encourage organic and inorganic chemical reactions that have a strong effect on plant growth, and fix nitrogen from the air in the soil. Most bacteria are found in the top one foot or so of soil.

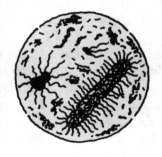

FUNGI: Fungi are multicelled and filamentous or single-celled primitive plants. They lack chlorophyll and therefore lack the ability to make their own carbohydrates. Fungi thrive mainly in well-drained, neutral to acidic, oxygenated soils. Mycorrhizal fungi helps the development of healthy root systems by growing on roots and effectively enlarging the length and surface area of roots. Some fungi are visible as white, cobweb-like threads that actually enter the cells of the root hairs.

MYCORRHIZAL FUNGI: Beneficial fungi that grow in or on the root systems of plants to increase their size and ability to access water and nutrients. These beneficial fungi live off exudates from plant roots. They will develop in healthy organic soil, but products such as Nature's Creation can be used to speed up their establishment.

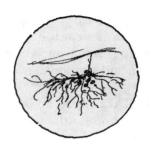

NEMATODES: Nematodes are probably the most numerous multicellular creatures on earth. They are active, tubular, microscopic animals living on moist surfaces or in liquid environments like the films of water in the soil. Destructive and beneficial nematodes exist in all soils. Some create knots on roots and some enter through lesions to feed on inside roots. Some species of beneficial nematodes are effective for the control of termites, grubworms, fire ants, fleas, and other pests. They will be present in healthy soils.

SLIME MOLDS: Amoeba-like organisms that live in damp rotting wood and leaves. They also grow on manure, lawn thatch, and other rotting organic material. They start off as individual organisms, but later form masses that look like slugs, jelly, or even vomit. Color will range from gray and tan to bright reds and yellows. Slime molds don't hurt anything unless they surround or completely cover small seedlings.

PROTOZOA: Protozoa are the simplest form of animals. They are single-celled and microscopic in size. They obtain their food from organic matter. Protozoa serve to regulate the size of the bacterial community.

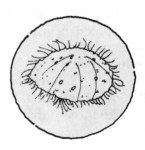

SOIL MACROORGANISMS

Healthy soil is not only full of billions of microorganisms, but it also contains many macroorganisms. These organisms can be seen with the naked eye. They range from tiny mites to large rodents and all have a specific function or purpose in the soil. The most famous and most helpful macroorganisms are the earthworms. Earthworms till and aerate the soil, increase drainage, stimulate microbiotic activity, and increase soil fertility. Healthy soil will have many earthworms.

There are three basic kinds of macroorganisms: herbivores, detritivores, and carnivores, although some may fit into more than one subgroup. Herbivores feed on living plants, detritivores feed on dead and decaying plant tissues, and carnivores feed on other living organisms (both micro and macroorganisms). Herbivores (plant eaters) include snails, slugs, insect larvae, termites, beetle larvae, woodchucks, mice, and grubs. Detritivores (decaying matter eaters) include mites, snails, beetles, millipedes, woodlice, springtails, earthworms, worms, spiders, scorpions, centipedes, earwigs, crickets, termites, slugs, and ants. Carnivores (animal eaters) include mites, springtails, enchytraeids, centipedes, snails, slugs, flies, moles, ants, spiders, centipedes, scorpions, and beetles.

Macroorganisms, the larger critters, loosen the soil by burrowing and digging, help decompose plant tissue for use by microorganisms, and help to create beneficial compounds that plants can use. As earthworms burrow up and down, they bring valuable minerals from deep in the soil up to the surface. These minerals are used by plants, and the burrowing helps oxygenate the root zone. Earthworms also take organic material from the surface and pull it down into the soil to help build the carbon storehouse.

While some macroorganisms can be considered harmful or destructive to plant roots, their presence may also be valuable to the health of the soil. For example, most grub worms only feed on dead and decaying matter, and all grubs aerate the soil. They may be an important food source for other organisms. The principles of organics teach that helping all pieces of nature work in harmony is essential. If we try to kill all the macroorganisms that are detrimental, we will certainly kill the beneficial ones as well. Balance in a healthy soil is the goal. When the balance is disrupted, the symptoms of insects and diseases attack plant crops.

MINERALS

The soil's most plentiful major component is mineral matter. In the top six inches of healthy soil, the mineral portion will be approximately 45 percent of the volume and is the principal determinant of the soil's property. Minerals occur as a result of the physical or chemical decomposition of the parent rock near the surface of the soil. Minerals are responsible for the growth of a plant's cells. Plants depend on three essential nutrients derived from carbon dioxide and water: carbon, hydrogen, and oxygen. Plants also depend on thirteen essential nutrients derived from the minerals in the soil as inorganic salts—iron, potassium, calcium, magnesium, nitrogen, phosphorous, sulfur, manganese, chlorine, boron, zinc, copper, and molybdenum. The other seventy or so trace minerals are not fully understood, but are important to the balance of healthy soil.

Organic fertilizers do not have very high amounts of nitrogen, phosphorous, and potassium. When fertilizing or adding mineral nutrients, it's important to think about balance. Healthy soils and plants have a balance of ingredients. A proper fertilization program will help keep that balance intact. That's why it's important to avoid an overkill of the well-known elements nitrogen, phosphorous, and potassium. Synthetic fertilizers are not balanced. They have too much nitrogen, no carbon and a poor collection of trace minerals.

Here's a good example. The following are the approximate percentages of various elements in whole plants:

Oxygen	45 percent
Carbon	44 percent
Hydrogen	6 percent
Nitrogen	2 percent
Potassium	1.1 percent
Phosphorous	0.4 percent
Sulfur	0.5 percent
Calcium	0.6 percent
Magnesium	0.3 percent

Note the relatively low percentages of nitrogen, phosphorous, and potassium and the high percentages of oxygen, carbon, and hydrogen.

When buying fertilizer, remember how relatively unimportant nitrogen, phosphorous, and potassium are. Think in terms of providing to the soil those ingredients that will help maintain the natural balance. If the soil is in a healthy, balanced condition (which includes plenty of organic matter and air), nitrogen, potassium, and phosphorous will be produced naturally by the feeding of microorganisms and relatively little will need to be added. Much of the N-P-K in synthetic fertilizer is not used by plants, but rather wasted to volatize and leach away to contaminate the environment.

FERTILIZER ELEMENTS

OXYGEN is an often overlooked element. Adding oxygen to most soils can cause an immediate response in plants, much the same effect as using high-nitrogen fertilizer. Oxygen can be added to the soil by mechanical means such as aerating, ripping, or tilling, but it also can be gotten indirectly by using organic fertilizers and soil conditioners. Healthy plants' extensive root systems can also be very beneficial for introducing oxygen into the all-important top twelve inches of soil.

NITROGEN is an essential constituent of proteins and vital to plant health. However, excessive nitrogen can cause an imbalance in plant metabolism, which can adversely affect plant growth, fruiting, and storage life.

Nitrogen is an ingredient of proteins and distinguishes them from carbohydrates. The amount of nitrogen in a given material is determined by dividing the percent of protein by 6.25. Cottonseed meal for example is 60 percent protein. Divide 60 by 6.25 equals 9.6 percent nitrogen. Unlike other nutrients, it does not originate from the soil, but from the air. Nitrogen enters the soil through rain or by being fixed by living organisms associated with legumes such as clover, peas, beans, and alfalfa. Some organisms such as blue-green algae can fix nitrogen without an association with plants. The air is approximately 80 percent nitrogen. Lack of vigor and yellowing of the oldest leaves are signs of nitrogen deficiency. Too much, or the wrong kind of nitrogen used on plants will actually cause insects and disease attacks by weakening and stressing the plants.

PHOSPHATE is the soil's catalyst. Its most important function is to help transfer the energy in the plant from one point to another. Adequate phosphorous is needed for color and vitality of the plant at bloom time and at maturity. It also helps increase seed and flower size. Soils must have sufficient levels of phosphates so that enough sugars are formed in the plants. Sources include: colloidal phosphate, superphosphate, rock phosphate, phosphoric acid, humate compost, greensand and rock powders. Deficiency characteristics are weak flower and fruit production. Healthy soil with mycorrhizal fungi will help make phosphorus available to plants.

CARBON is the main energy source in the soil. It is essential for the availability of nitrogen and phosphate and is critical for healthy microorganisms. Between 45 and 56 percent of a plant's compounds contain carbon. Sources of carbon include compost, manures, humates, molasses, organic fertilizers, and natural mulches.

CALCIUM is the king of the nutrients. It is the most critical in low humus soils. Calcium is needed to feed the microbes and affect the permeability of plant cell walls and the thickness of stems. Sources include: lime (calcitic limestone or calcium carbonate), gypsum, marl, and dolomitic lime (which is the worst choice for some soil because of the presence of magnesium). Calcium deficiency characteristics include die-back of growth tips in tops, generally poor growth and roots and increased susceptibility to disease.

HYDROGEN is a nonmetallic element that is the simplest and lightest of all and is one of the three most plentiful elements in plants. It is flammable and the most abundant element in the universe. Hydrogen combines with oxygen to form water (H_2O) and hydrogen peroxide (H_2O_2).

MAGNESIUM has more effect on pH than calcium does. It is important for photosynthesis and helps hold the soil together. Magnesium aids in phosphate metabolism. Plants will show a deficiency if there is too much or too little magnesium. Deficiency will cause thin leaves and yellowing between veins from the bottom of the plant up. Sources include: Sul-Po-Mag (K-Mag), Epsom salts (magnesium sulfate), magnesium oxide, and compost.

POTASSIUM or potash is a metabolic regulator and is essential to the balance between leaf and root growth and necessary for winter and summer hardiness. This element exists in ample quantities in many soils but is often tied up due to mineral imbalance. Sources include: granite, greensand, potassium sulfate, Sul-Po-Mag, molasses, and compost. Deficiency characteristics include early winter-kill, poor survival of perennials, and increased susceptibility to disease.

SULFUR, called secondary, is actually a major element. Like nitrogen, a deficiency causes yellow leaves, but a nitrogen deficiency affects the older leaves first. Sulfur deficiency turns the newest leaves yellow. Sulfur is the easiest leached of all minerals. It can be used in alkaline soils to help balance the availability of calcium and magnesium. Sulfur improves the taste of food, increases protein content, and promotes seed production. Sources include compost, molasses, sulfates, elemental sulfur, gypsum, compost, and garlic products.

CHLORIDE is needed in balanced soils, although excessive amounts can be a great problem in the soil. Sources include city-treated water, fish products and compost.

SODIUM has an important relationship with potassium. The available potassium must be higher than the available sodium. Adequate amounts of sodium help to prevent diseases. Sources include most manures, baking soda, organic fertilizers, fish products, and compost.

BORON is important for nitrogen efficiency and disease resistance and allows the use of less nitrogen. Deficiencies show up as purple leaves, reduced sugar content, bitter taste, cracks in root crops, and corkiness. Boron exists in all cell membranes and is important for nitrogen fixation. Boron works closely with calcium and contributes more than any other micronutrient to the quality of produce. Other deficiency symptoms included: tip growth die back, light green buds, roots brown in the center, and flowers that don't form properly. Boron is also important for disease resistance. Sources include borates, fish meal and compost. Caution—it is very easy to use too much and cause boron toxicity.

IRON is an essential element for photosynthesis and for the green color in plants. Deficiency shows up as yellow on youngest leaves from top to bottom (veins, margins, and tips stay green). Iron and other trace minerals are often tied up in calcareous soils. Sources include copperas (ferrous sulfate), chelated iron, several organic fertilizers, and greensand. Greensand is an especially good source.

MANGANESE deficiency shows up as white tissue between the veins. Plants will be dwarfed and leaves will have dead spots. If sodium plus potassium equals 10 percent or more of the available nutrients, no manganese will get to the plant. Deficiency symptoms are similar to those from lack of iron. Sources include manganese sulfates, chelates, organic fertilizers, fish products, and compost.

COPPER is an important micronutrient for disease resistance. Most soils are deficient in copper. One reason is that too much nitrogen ties up copper. Most common sources are copper sulfate, organic fertilizers, fish products, and compost.

ZINC availability requires a well-aerated soil and is important for the sweet taste in vegetables and fruit. Deficiency shows in leaves with dead areas, poor bud formation, and small terminal leaves. Weed pressure is greater when zinc is deficient. Sources include kelp meal, fish products, liquid seaweed, zinc sulfate, organic fertilizers and compost.

MOLYBDENUM is important in natural nitrogen fixation but usually unavailable in acid soils. Healthy plants will usually have between .01 and 10 ppm. Other than being important for the health of certain microbes, there is much mystery about the importance of molybdenum. Sources include most all organic fertilizers, fish products, humates, and compost.

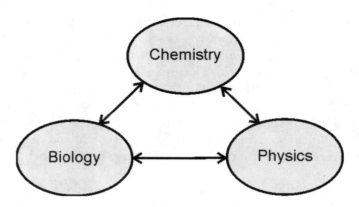

The health, balance, and productivity of the soil depend on three basic pieces being in place: chemistry, biology, and physics. They are all three dependent upon each other. The soil's chemistry must be balanced for the physics and biology to be correct. The living portion of the soil must be healthy for the tilth and drainage to work properly, and the physical properties of the soil must be correct for the living organisms to thrive. Nature will balance the soil for you over time if a few basic ingredients are added and maintained: organic matter, air, and moisture. Other organic amendments simply speed up the process.

BASIC ORGANIC PROGRAM

HOW PLANTS GROW

Sunlight is the source of all energy. Green leaves are the instruments for gathering in sunlight. Sunlight energy and the gas called carbon dioxide (CO_2) enter the foliage of plants to combine with water and chlorophyll to form sugars, proteins, fats, and carbohydrates—the food stuff of plants. This process is known as *photosynthesis*. This naturally created food is transferred from the foliage through the stems and limbs down through the trunk into the roots and out into the soil in the form of exudates. Exudates in the form of dead cells and gel-like materials leave the roots through the root hairs and enter the rhizosphere to feed beneficial soil microorganisms.

The rhizosphere is the soil area that is immediately adjacent to the roots. It is the location of the heaviest concentration of microbiotic activity. Some of the beneficial soil microorganisms include: mycorrhizal fungi, nitrogen-fixing bacteria, yeasts, algae, cyanobacteria, actinomycetes, protozoa, mites, beneficial nematodes, and other small animals. Here the roots and soil are working together to produce and release nutrients to feed the plant.

Microorganisms of all sorts feed on the soil's energy-rich substances, releasing a vast array of minerals, vitamins, antibiotics, regulators, enzymes, and other compounds that can be absorbed into the roots and taken back into the plant to produce strong growth and increased pest and disease resistance. Roots take up nutrients from the soil and pass them up into the plant, causing stem and leaf top growth.

Whether the plant is a bluebonnet, bur oak, or blue grass, this natural process is the same and only works at its full potential and efficiency if the soil is healthy. That can only happen in the absence of synthetic fertilizers and toxic chemical pesticides.

HOW TO START AN ORGANIC PROGRAM

The interest and enthusiasm over organic farming, ranching, and gardening is spreading rapidly. My most often-asked question is, "How do I get started?"

Organic agriculture, gardening, and landscaping all have the same basic philosophy of working with nature's system to maintain the soil, food crops, and ornamental plants without synthetic fertilizers or toxic chemical pesticides.

Organic fertilizers stimulate soil microorganisms and earthworms, provide humus, and help to aerate the soil. They also provide major nutrients—nitrogen, phosphorous, and potash, as well as secondary nutrients—calcium, sulfur, and magnesium, and many trace elements such as copper, zinc, boron, manganese, and molybdenum. In addition, organic techniques help to save water by allowing soils to drain well while maintaining proper moisture levels for longer periods of time. The exudates from the microbes in the soil are primarily responsible for this condition.

Natural organic programs work with nature's laws and systems rather than try to fight and control nature as chemical programs and products try to do.

I'm reluctant to say it's easy because anything new seems hard at first, especially when a completely new thought process is required, but the natural way really is better in every way. Conventional horticulture and ag programs are based on force-feeding plants and killing pests with harsh nonselective poisons. Organic programs are based on encouraging health and working within nature's laws to help her control life the natural way.

The heart of organics is soil improvement. Healthy soil produces healthy plants with very powerful natural insect and disease resistance.

If you are ready to start your natural organic program, here's how it works.

SEVEN STEPS IN GOING ORGANIC

1. Make Good Plant Decisions — Stop catching the grass clippings. Allow the clippings to return to the soil. Use native plants when possible or well-adapted introductions. Always use the well-adapted plants for specific environments. Plant annuals in the proper season and use diversity in your plantings. If you don't use adapted plants, the rest of rules will do little good.

2. Stop Using Toxic Chemicals — Stop harming the soil life. There are millions of types of insects and microbes, but only a small percentage are considered harmful, the others are known to be beneficial. Pesticides and harsh synthetic fertilizers hurt or kill both. Two big lies exist and control the industry. These lies have been in power since just after World War II. Before that time, gardeners, farmers, and ranchers did a pretty good job of using organic techniques—that's all they had. Yes, even in those days much of the land was "worn out" by over producing and that mistake caused people to move on to fresh, productive land. The cause was ignorance of the importance of replenishing what's taken away from the soil in the form of crops and what literally vaporizes by tilling and leaving the soil bare. Carbon escapes as carbon dioxide when the land is left bare and/or tilled too often.

Big Lie Number 1. "Plants can't tell the difference between organic and synthetic fertilizers." Well, yes they can. The traditional argument is that plants can only take in fertilizer elements in the basic or ion form. It's a silly notion. These same people will instantly agree that plants take in water—H_2O is a molecule, not an ion. Plants do not take in H and O ions. To make the example more dramatic, water a white flowering plant with blue, red, or any color dye. The color will move easily into the plant and discolor the flower. Is the dye a basic element or ion? Of course not, it's a very large molecule. One more—herbicides that enter plants and kill by interfering with the normal cellular growth are not ions, they are huge, complex molecules. What do they do—disassemble into carbon, hydrogen and oxygen, enter the plant and then reassemble? It would be a funny thought except that this inane comment is often made in total seriousness. Dr. Bargyla Rateaver's books not only explain how plants absorb chunks of materials, including whole bacteria, they have electron microscope photos of the process in action.

There are other differences as well. Organic fertilizers, whether they are meals, manures or composted plant material, contain N-P-K, trace minerals, enzymes, vitamins, and lots of organic matter. 100 percent of each bag's ingredients is useful to the soil and plants. Artificial fertilizers are primarily water soluble mineral salts and phosphorous. There are rarely very many trace minerals included and usually zero organic matter. Some of the synthetic fertilizers have sulfur or polymers to slow down the release process—a move in the right direction but the organic products all have natural slow release. A large percentage of the synthetic fertilizers leach through to soil to contaminate the water supply.

One more problem, a large percentage of each bag of artificial fertilizers is a mystery. For example, one of the most commonly recommended fertilizers has an analysis of 15-5-10 (the 3-1-2 ratio that's commonly touted). Those numbers stand for nitrogen, phosphorous, and potassium. This particular fertilizer contains 15 percent nitrogen, 5 percent phosphorus, and 10 percent potassium— adds up to 30 percent. OK—what's the other 70 percent of that bag of fertilizer? Beats me, too. That's the problem. Believe it or not, most states, including Texas, do not regulate the inert ingredients in fertilizers, and basically anything can be used, including industrial waste and heavy metals. How do you know for sure? Simple—ask the supplier to give you a total analysis. You might notice their knees buckle a little. Although some of the artificial stuff is very clean, I still don't recommend it. Most artificial fertilizers feed plants too fast and a glut of nitrogen causes weak cells and plants that are more susceptible to insects and diseases. Yes, the plants can tell the difference.

The 2nd Big Lie — "Toxic chemical pesticides are necessary to control pests and perfectly safe when used according to label directions." I spend my life these days explaining this in detail, but here's the concept in a nutshell. If pesticides worked, this lie might not be so bad—however, there is more money spent today on pesticides than ever before, yet about one-third of all food crops are still lost to pest insects. That's the same percentage as before the pesticides became available. Toxic pesticides kill beneficial insects and beneficial microorganisms. They also damage the frogs, toads, lizards, birds, bats, and other good guys. The irony is that these high tech pesticides damage the animals that provide powerful natural pest control. Furthermore, healthy soil produces healthy plants that have a natural insect and disease resistance. Adapted plants that are planted in soil full of compost, rock powders, living organisms, and available nutrients are not in stress and don't attract insect pests and pathogenic microorganisms.

3. Build Soil Organic Matter Content — Start using compost, rock powders, sugars, and natural organic fertilizers. Use compost to prepare beds and gardens and apply natural organic fertilizers. Nature has built and maintained fertile soil since the beginning of time in the forests and on prairies through a constant recycling of dead plant and animal life. Stimulation of microbiotic activity in the soil is the most important way of building soil organic matter. The waste materials and dead bodies of microbes are the most common source of organic matter (humus). Aerating the soil can speed up this process.

Increase the air in the soil through mechanical aeration when needed. Liquid bio-stimulants and/or living organism products can serve the same function. Use deeply rooted cover crops, encourage earthworms, add compost, and mulch all bare soil. All life needs oxygen, and that includes the soil microorganisms. The sticky substance given off by healthy microbes as they break down organic materials glues the soil into a crumb structure creating the perfect air-to-soil ratio.

Mulch the bare soil. Nature doesn't allow bare soil and neither should we. For shrubs, trees, and ground covers, use at least one inch of compost and three inches of shredded tree trimmings. Partially completed compost is also an excellent topdressing material. Natural mulch preserves moisture, helps to eliminate weeds, and keeps the soil surface cooler, which benefits earthworms, microorganism, and plant roots. Do not pile mulch onto the stems or trunks of plants, however.

4. Build Mineral Content of the Soil — Add finely crushed volcanic rock to all planting beds, lawns, and gardens. Nature has maintained the mineral balance through volcanic eruptions, glaciers movement, and bed rock erosion. Don't worry about pH. When a balance of natural materials are used, pH will move to the correct level. Additional volcanic rock is not needed in volcanic soils. Useful products include lava sand, basalt, zeolite, and also nonvolcanic rock such as humates, rock phosphates, and other rock material that is different from the base rock on the property.

5. Use the Least Toxic Pest Control Products Available — Choose repellents and biological products first since they don't hurt beneficial insects and other life. Avoid even the toxic organic pesticides like pyrethrum and rotenone. Toxic pesticides control pests poorly. Because they are indiscriminate and kill more beneficials than pests, they actually make insect and disease problems worse. The sellers of toxic pesticides are the only ones who benefit from their use.

6. Encourage Biodiversity — Encourage life and biodiversity by introducing beneficial insects and protecting those that exist. Plant cover crops and hedgerows. Purchase and release ladybugs, green lacewings, and trichogramma wasps. You'll need to buy less every year because natural populations will establish.

7. Water Wisely — Irrigation should be done thoroughly and deeply, but less often. Healthy soil that results from the organic program holds moisture at the right level for a longer period of time. Overwatering is one of the most serious mistakes made in landscaping and farming.

Troublesome insects, diseases, and weeds are symptoms of one of the above rules being violated. Using pesticides only treats the symptoms. Pests are the effects of deeper problems. However, most of the research time and money has been foolishly spent on treating symptoms and ignoring the cause. Don't be one of the foolish. Please remember that you are dealing with living soil, living plants, and other living creatures. Nature is dynamic and always changing. No program is the best for everyone, so start out with my program and then fine-tune it into your own. No single organic program is perfect—except for nature's own.

Here's the shorthand version of the program:
1. Stop using all synthetic pesticides and other toxic chemicals.
2. Build soil health with natural organic products and techniques.
3. Use native plants and well-adapted introductions.

BUILDING A HEALTHY SOIL

Building a healthy soil is done by putting the basic elements in place and letting Mother Nature do the rest. Most unhealthy soils lack air and humus, have a weak population of microorganisms, and are chemically unbalanced. All these things are related, and improving any one of them indirectly improves the others.

The first step in major soil improvement is to aerate the ground. Cultivated and pasture land can be ripped or chisel plowed, and turf areas should be mechanically aerated. Ornamental beds should be aerated with a turning fork or hand aerated. My favorite tools for the home gardener are in The Perfect Garden Tool System. Liquid microorganism products can also be used to increase the oxygen in the soil.

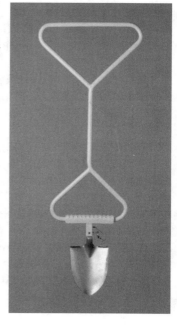

Balanced soil has approximately the following breakdown.

Oxygen	4-5%
Humus	2.5-5.0%
Calcium	65-75%
Magnesium	12-20%
Potassium	3-7.5%
Phosphate	250-375 PPM
Sulfate	25-50 PPM
Nitrogen	20-40 PPM
Sodium	0.5-3.0%
Salt	400 PPM or less
Chlorides	80-120 PPM
Boron	0.8-2.0 PPM
Iron	200 PPM or more
Manganese	50-125 PPM
Copper	2-5 PPM
Zinc	10-20 PPM

% = percentage of available nutrients
PPM = parts per million

RECREATING THE FOREST FLOOR

The next step in becoming organic is to recreate the forest floor in all your beds, veggie gardens, and ornamental gardens. Pastures and turf also need to have the components of the forest floor.

A natural forest floor cross section looks like this: the top two to four inches are mulch—leaves, twigs, bark, dead plants, dead bodies of animals, and animal manure. Below that is one to two inches of one-year-old organic matter and well broken-down humus. Below that is a mixture of humus and the rock particles of the area. Minerals are contained in the humus and in the broken-up pieces of the base rock material.

Below that is the subsoil. Earthworms, insects, and roots are mixed all throughout the layers. The top seven inches of the forest floor is the area that is the most well-aerated and host to the bulk of soil biology. That layered structure, transitioning down from rough mulch to subsoil, is exactly what we want to create in the vegetable garden and in the ornamental garden.

This very definite layering of rough mulch on top of humus and native soil is nature's way of covering, protecting, and stimulating the soil. Why then should we not do the same thing in our cultivated gardens? Nowhere in the wild will Mother Nature allow the ground to be bare, except for deserts and naturally eroded areas.

There are several ways to create a manmade "forest floor." The easiest way is to take the leaves from your own property or from the plastic bags unenlightened neighbors have left along the street and dump them onto bare areas in the planting beds. The depth of this raw material can range from eight to twelve inches. This easy method can also be done with clean hay, tree trimmings mulch, and most any raw organic material. Fine-textured matter such as sawdust, if used at all, should be applied in thinner layers since there is less air space between the small pieces and, therefore, less oxygen and carbon dioxide exchange at the soil surface. It's better to compost fine-textured materials such as sawdust or other fresh materials before using them on the beds. Raw sawdust can also rob nitrogen from the soil.

A better way to create the "forest floor" is to use partially completed compost. The texture of the material will be better and the resulting improvement to the soil will be faster. Partially completed compost means you can still identify a portion of the raw materials. The texture is better because a mix of large and small particles and decomposed particles will exist. Soil improvement will be faster because of the high population of beneficial microorganisms. I use partially completed compost (living mulch) as mulch at a depth of two to four inches.

To go a step farther, apply a layer of completed compost on the bare soil at a depth of one to two inches and cover the compost with a thick blanket (three to four inches) of shredded native tree trimmings, hardwood bark, pine needles, or clean hay. Pine bark can be used, but it is my least favorite choice because its flat pieces can plate to seal off oxygen and it can move around easily from wind and water.

My favorite mulch is living mulch, or partially composted shredded native tree trimmings. I do not recommend mulches made from paper, plastic, rubber, or gravel unless you have no source of natural vegetative materials. Various mulching methods will work to keep the soil temperature and moisture correct, prevent wind and water erosion, and stimulate the life in the soil. Covering the bare soil with mulch is probably the single most important aspect of organic gardening.

Here's the ideal way to replicate the "forest floor."

STEP 1: Aerate by punching holes in the ground.

STEP 2: Spray the soil with compost tea, seaweed, or some biological stimulator. Garrett Juice is the best single product to use.

STEP 3: Apply a light coating of finished compost—just enough to barely cover the soil. Earthworm casting can be used for this.

STEP 4: Apply a two-to-four-inch layer of shredded nature tree trimmings mulch.

Note: As a precaution, do not pile mulch up onto the trunks of plants. If the mulch is kept constantly wet, it can girdle trees.

We'll never be able to do as good a job as Mother Nature in creating the forest floor, but we can come pretty close.

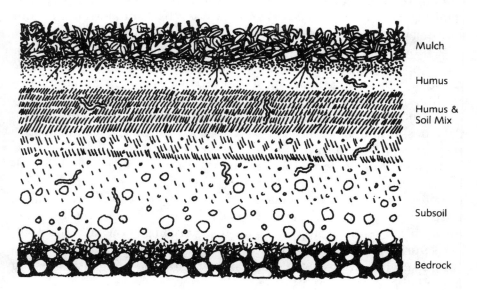

Mulch

Humus

Humus & Soil Mix

Subsoil

Bedrock

The forest floor soil cross section consists of mulch or litter on the surface, decayed organic matter or humus, followed by minerals and humus mixed, followed by subsoil and bedrock.

BIODIVERSITY

I'm a very lucky person. In 1987, I met a fellow who not only became a friend, but introduced me to the organic way of life. Malcolm Beck, a longtime organic gardener and farmer from San Antonio, taught me how to make compost. He also taught me that every living thing will sooner or later die and everything that dies rots and recycles its nutrients and energy back into the soil. On the surface, that sounds pretty morbid, doesn't it? In reality, it is fundamental to understanding life, nature, and organics. If dead things didn't rot, this earth would be several thousand feet deep in dead bodies and a smelly place indeed. Malcolm taught me that the decaying process returns the dead plants and animals back to the earth and into the raw elements from which they were made. These basic mineral elements in their journey back become the nutrition and vitality to feed the next generation of plants, animals, and man. The decaying process is performed by the billions of little creatures in the soil we call microorganisms or microbes. They will do their job with or without our help. In fact, it is almost impossible to stop them. The microorganisms can turn our once-alive organic waste back into fertilizer for our farms, lawns, and gardens. They can, that is, if they are allowed to do so.

Unfortunately, in most cities, vegetative waste such as leaves, grass clippings and tree trimmings are usually buried in landfills where these life-sustaining nutrients are locked away from air and the natural life, death, and decay cycle. What could have been a great benefit to the fertility and well-being of the soil has become a great problem. All cities should make it illegal to send grass clippings, shrub and tree trimmings to the landfill.

Dead organic material can be managed into a financial and horticultural benefit. All we have to do is protect, encourage, and stimulate microorganisms and friends like beneficial insects, frogs, toads, lizards, snakes, birds, and other critical parts of what we lump together into the term *biodiversity*. It's simple. Stop killing the living organisms on and in the soil!

Nature is not a bunch of independent pieces. Nature is a whole. It is a complete whole where everything is related to everything else. Hurting any small part of nature hurts everything and everyone.

All living organisms die and they all rot, and everything that rots provides food and life for the next phase of life. Your compost pile will show this quite clearly if you just watch.

PLANT DECISIONS

SELECTING ORNAMENTALS

Books exist in most any region of the country that recommend and explain the best plants to use. Using the native plants of a particular region is becoming more popular and this practice fits well with an organic program. There are also adapted plants that have been introduced from other parts of the world. I prefer native plants when possible, but the key is to use varieties that will like their new home, making them easy to grow and economical to maintain. In most cases, natives are well adapted and have developed resistance to most harmful insects. Centuries of natural selection have given native plants the ability to survive without pesticides or high levels of fertilization, particularly if they are grown in a healthy soil.

Nature doesn't allow monocultures. Neither should landscape architects or gardeners. When choosing plants (native or introduced), select a variety so that insects and harmful microorganisms will not have one target group. Look at what has happened to millions of American elm trees all over the United States to understand why a diversity of plants is best in the long run. Large monoculture plantings have been devastated.

Another reason to use well-adapted plants in the landscape is water usage and conservation. Water conservation becomes a more serious issue each year and the careful selection of plant materials can make a significant impact on irrigation needs since water requirements vary greatly from plant to plant.

Of course I recommend *Plants for Texas, Texas Organic Vegetable Gardening,* and *Texas Gardening-The Natural Way* for Texas, but similar books exist in other parts of the country. Do yourself a big favor by spending some time at your local bookstore, nursery, library, county agent, urban forester's office, or local college or university, learning about the best plants for your area. Then select a variety of plants that will meet your aesthetic and horticultural needs. In conjunction with the organic practices discussed in this book, you should then have the basics for creating a beautiful landscape, requiring only a minimal amount of maintenance. Note the recommended reading list in the appendix of this book.

My best advice for the selection of trees, shrubs, vines, ground covers, and flowers is to invest in all the local reference books and get the free literature from the botanical gardens, zoos, park departments, and civic garden clubs. Talk to several nurseries and look at the plants you are considering in different landscape situations. Don't be afraid to try some experiments, but build the framework of the landscape with tough, pest-resistant, adapted varieties.

LANDSCAPING WITH HERBS

They have been planted for years for their culinary and medicinal uses, but now there's growing interest in another use. Herbs make wonderful landscape plants. Many are drought tolerant and grow in almost any well-drained soil. They provide color, texture, and wonderful fragrances. Herbs also give us help with insect control and make excellent companion plants for our vegetable and ornamental plant materials. They fit perfectly into an organic program because they should only be fertilized with natural fertilizers and they should never be sprayed with pesticides.

There are bush-type herbs such as salvia and rosemary. There are excellent groundcovers like creeping thyme and pennyroyal mint. There are many beautiful flowering varieties such as yarrow and sweet marigold. Herbs also have effective insect controlling qualities. Here are some of my favorite herbs to use as landscape plants. I'm not pooh-poohing the medicinal and culinary uses—quite the contrary—I just like for you to have something else to think about.

BASIL *(Ocimum* spp.) is available in many types of purple and green basil, and they all make excellent annual plants to use as borders or low masses. Plant from seed or transplants in sun or partial shade. They will usually return from seed each year, but if they don't, buy some more.

BORAGE *(Borago officinalis)* is a beautiful, soft herb that grows to about three feet tall. The leaves are gray-green and have whitish bristles. The flowers are star shaped and peacock blue and bloom throughout the summer. Plant in sun or partial shade.

CATNIP *(Nepeta cataria)* is a tall ground cover or shrubby perennial with gray-green, oval leaves. It will reach about three feet in height. It has small, white or lavender flowers and is excellent for attracting bees and butterflies—and cats, unfortunately. Sun or partial shade.

CHIVES *(Allium schoenoprasum)* grow in clumps and look a little bit like monkey grass. Onion chives have lavender flowers and round leaves. Garlic chives *(A. tuberosum)* have white flowers and flat leaves. Sun or partial shade.

COMFREY *(Symphytum officinale):* The "healing herb" has large, hairy, ten-to-fifteen-inch-long leaves. The plant will spread to three feet high by three feet wide and has lovely, bell-shaped flowers in pink and purple shades that hang gracefully from the stems and last throughout most of the summer. It can grow in sun or shade and should be used as an accent plant or in a large massing. Comfrey will stay evergreen during mild winters but always comes back and establishes into a hardy perennial.

DITTANY OF CRETE *(Origanum dictamnus)* is an excellent herb for hanging baskets or patio containers. It has small, soft, round, gray leaves and tiny purple flowers summer through fall. Best in full sun.

GARLIC *(Allium sativum):* Of course, we have to have garlic to eat and to ward off the "evil eye" and the bulbs to make the garlic tea, but it is also a good-looking landscape plant. The foliage of garlic is dark green and the flowers are very interesting as they curve around and finally burst open in the early summer. Best in full sun but can take some shade.

SCENTED GERANIUMS *(Pelargonium* spp.) are excellent landscape plants because of the lovely texture and the delicate flowers, but, more importantly, the fragrance when rubbed against or crushed. They come in all sizes and all leaf shapes including deeply cut leaves and those that are soft and velvety. Use in sun to partial shade.

ELDERBERRY *(Sambucus canadensis)* is a large-growing, beautiful perennial that is often grown for its edible purple-black berries in August through September. It can grow to a height of ten to twelve feet in most soils and has lovely white flower clusters in the summer. It is also noted for its ability to produce very fine humus soil in the root zone and is a wonderful plant for attracting birds. Sun to part shade. Can be a little messy.

GARDEN SAGE *(Salvia officinalis)* is a very tough, evergreen perennial with grayish-green leaves. The only negative is that it will develop woody growth after a while and need to be replaced. There are several different selections including some that have variegated foliage. Plant in sun or part shade, don't overwater and cut back once in the later winter or early spring.

LAMB'S EAR *(Stachys byzantina)* is a tough, fuzzy-leafed, gray herb that makes an excellent ground cover to contrast with darker green plants. It can take full sun up to some fairly heavy shade. Lamb's ear's velvet-like foliage and lavender blossoms that are delightful to see and to touch. Needs full sun.

LEMON BALM *(Melissa officinalis)* is an easy-to-grow, fragrant herb with leaves that are light green and oval with scalloped edges. It has a lemony fragrance and is excellent to interplant among vegetable and landscape plants to look good, help repel pests, and attract bees. Be careful—it can be invasive. Sun or part shade.

LEMONGRASS *(Cybopogon citratus):* is an herb that looks like pampas grass. It grows to a height of about three feet, has a wonderful lemon scent, and is excellent for making tea. Although it rarely flowers, it has a pleasant texture for a specimen landscape plant. It freezes above zone 8 so just plant a new one each year. Best in full sun, but can take some shade.

LEMON VERBENA *(Aloysia triphylla)* is a wonderfully fragrant addition to the landscape garden as well as the herb garden. It is sensitive to cold so it's best treated as an annual although it can be used in a pot and brought indoors during the cold months. Best in full sun.

MEXICAN MINT MARIGOLD *(Tagetes lucida):* (See Sweet marigold).

MINT *(Mentha* spp.) Mints of all kinds make good landscape ground covers, but be careful—they all spread aggressively. *Mentha pulegium* is pennyroyal and is an good landscape ground cover and reported to repel fleas. Sun or partial shade.

MULLEIN *(Verbascum thapsus):* Common mullein is a wildflower that looks like a large version of lamb's ear, but is more upright and has larger foliage. It also has yellow, white, or purple flowers depending on the variety. Also called flannel leaf or old man's flannel, mullein is a distinctive specimen plant to use in the garden. Full sun to partial shade.

PERILLA *(Perilla frutescens)* is an easy-to-grow annual with dark burgundy or green leaves. Growth habits are similar to that of coleus or basil. In fact, it looks a great deal like opal basil. However, it can spread aggressively. It can be planted from seed or from transplants and will reseed easily each year. It looks beautiful in contract with gray plants such as dusty miller, wormwood, or southernwood. Sun or partial shade.

PINEAPPLE SAGE *(Salvia elegans)* has beautiful, red flowers in the late summer or fall. It perennializes in mild winters, but should be considered an annual for most of the country in sun or shade.

ROSEMARY *(Rosmarinus officinalis)* is a beautiful, dark green shrub that can grow to a height of four feet. It will freeze in hard winters, but it is worth replanting every year if necessary. Rosemary has a marvelous pinelike fragrance and beautiful light blue flowers. The low-growing groundcover type is *Rosemary prostratus*.

SAFFRON *(Crocus sativus):* The true saffron is an autumn-blooming crocus that resembles ordinary crocus. It has lavender flowers that show in the fall. The saffron food flavor is made from the red-orange stigmas of the plant. It's easy to grow, but very labor intensive to harvest.

SALAD BURNET *(Poterium sanguisorba)* is a compact evergreen herb that will reach two feet tall with a rosette shape. The plant provides a pleasant cucumber fragrance and has flowers that form on long stems growing out of the center of the plant. Its lacy, symmetrical shape and nice texture make it a good accent plant. Sun or part shade.

SOUTHERNWOOD *(Artemisia abrotanum)* has delicate-looking, dusty-gray foliage that emits a lemon scent even when uncrushed but stronger when crushed. Full sun is best.

SWEET MARIGOLD or Mexican Mint Marigold *(Tagetes lucida)* is a substitute for French tarragon and much easier to grow. It has a strong fragrance in the garden and produces a terrific display of yellow-orange blossoms in the late summer and early fall.

TANSY *(Tanacetum vulgare)* is an easy-to-grow, ferny-leafed herb that blooms with yellow, button-like flowers in the late summer to early fall. Crushed or chopped tansy leaves emit a very bitter taste and are an excellent repellant for ants. Sun or part shade, but best in sun.

THYME *(Thymus vulgaris)* makes an excellent landscape plant, especially the creeping thyme, which makes a beautiful and extremely fragrant groundcover that is particularly effective between stepping stones and on borders. Creeping thyme also works well on retaining walls to flow down over the wall. Full sun is best.

WORMWOOD *(Artemisia* spp.) is another gray-leafed plant that is extremely drought tolerant and is a nice contrast with darker plants. Best in full sun.

YARROW *(Achillea millifolum)* is a very lacy, fern-like evergreen perennial with colorful flowers on tall stalks that bloom in the early summer in white, pinks and reds. Best in full sun. Top dies back completely in northern climates.

Most herbs will do best in well-drained beds made from a mix of compost, rock minerals, and native soil. The best location is full sun in morning and at least some protection from the hot afternoon sun.

It's amazing how old-fashioned things like organics and herbs have come back so strongly. The reason is simple—they work so well.

Herbs also have effective insecticidal qualities. Here are some of my favorites that can be planted among the other vegetable and ornamental plants to help ward off the listed pests.

Herb	Pests Warded Off
Basil	Flies and mosquitoes
Borage	Tomato worm
Garlic	Aphids, beetles, weevils, borers, spider mites
Henbit	Most insects
Lamium	Potato bugs
Marigold	Many insects
Nasturtium	Aphids, squash bugs, white fly
Pennyroyal	Ants, aphids, ticks, fleas
Peppermint	Ants
Pyrethrum	Most insects
Rosemary	Cabbage moths, beetles, mosquitoes, and slugs
Rue	Beetles
Sage	Moths
Spearmint	Ants, aphids
Thyme	Cabbage worms and many other insects
Lavender	Ants
Tansy	Ants
Onion	Cabbage moths

VEGETABLES, FRUITS, NUTS

To make the best selection, check with the local extension service, local growers, nurseries, and especially local gardeners. Plant a diverse mix of varieties, but try to stick with the toughest and most adapted. An excellent source of information will usually be local organic growers and experienced home gardeners. No matter what vegetables you plant, be sure to prepare well-drained and highly organic beds, plant in the proper season, and put a thick mulch layer over all bare soil.

No matter what food crops you decide to try, remember that, in most cases, these plants are probably not native to your area. For that reason, it's imperative to loosen the soil to provide plenty of oxygen and add lots of compost for additional humus.

Use natural organic fertilizers liberally if the soil is not biologically active. Also add liberal amounts of rock powders and molasses. Supplement the soil treatments by spraying regularly with Garrett Juice. Effective rock powders include rock phosphate, greensand, granite, and glacial rock dust. Micronized (fine textured) products are fast acting and very effective.

Keep all bare soil mulched at all times, except when new seeds are coming up. Alfalfa hay is the best mulch for vegetable gardens and should be applied eight inches thick to allow for settling. Bermuda should be used very carefully. Much of it contains broad leaf herbicides that can damage or kill crops. Partially composted native tree trimmings are excellent mulches for all kinds of plantings.

The most common recommendation is to water by drip irrigation and avoid wetting the foliage too often. Water infrequently but deeply when needed. I admit to still watering by sprinkling. I like to see where the water is going. Drip systems can cause dry spots and spots that are supersaturated.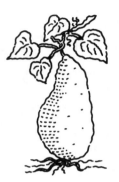

Control insect pests by releasing beneficial insects and by hand removal. Problem infestations can be controlled with various organic pest control products. Check the pest control section starting on page 91 for further details.

WILDFLOWERS

Wildflowers have always been popular in the wild, at least for those people taking the time to stop for a moment and look at them. On the other hand, many people have become frustrated over trying to establish wildflowers on their own properties. Growing wildflowers can be fairly easy, but it isn't as simple as throwing seed on the ground and waiting for the spring show. Once again, we need to watch what works in nature and try to use those techniques and even improve on them where possible.

Here are some tips to help give you a better chance of a beautiful display of wildflower color next spring.

1. **Timing:** The time to plant is late spring through summer. Sowing the seed in late spring best duplicates when nature scatters seed on the earth. The seed probably need the heat and ultraviolet rays for proper germination. Fall is the second best time.

2. **Soil Preparation:** Begin by raking bare soil to a depth of no more than one inch. Deep tilling is not only a waste of money, but can actually damage the soil and encourage weeds. If grass or weeds exist in the planting site you've chosen, set the mower on its lowest setting and scalp the area down to bare soil.

3. **Planting:** Mist or soak the seed in liquid humate or compost tea. I use Garrett Juice. Next, distribute the seed uniformly over the area at the recommended rate and rake lightly into the soil to assure good soil/seed contact. It's not essential but is ideal to broadcast a thin (one-quarter inch) layer of compost over the seeded area. Water the seeded area thoroughly, but be careful to avoid overwatering, which will erode the loose soil and displace the seed. Many of the wildflower varieties will germinate in the fall, and the small plants will be visible all winter. Others will only start to be visible the next spring.

4. **Maintenance:** The most critical step in wildflower planting is to help Mother Nature with the watering if needed. Be sure to provide irrigation (it can be temporary irrigation) the first fall if it is a dry season and again in March and April if it's an unusually dry spring. This is a critical step. The tiny plants need moisture as they germinate and start to grow. They will survive in low water settings once established, but they need moisture to get started. The only fertilization I recommend is a light application of earthworm castings, compost, humate, or other 100 percent organic fertilizer after the seeds germinate and begin to grow in the early spring. Or, just depend on Mother Nature to take care of things.

5. **Selection:** Some wildflowers are easier to grow than others. On the following page are the ones I would recommend for the beginner. This list will provide a long display and a wide variety of colors.

Wildflower	Scientific Name	Colors
Black-eyed Susan	*(Rudbeckia hirta)*	yellow
Bluebonnet	*(Lupinus texensis)*	blue
Butterfly weed	*(Asclepia tuberosa)*	orange
Coreopsis	*(C. lanceolata)*	yellow
Coreopsis	*(C. tinctoria)*	red & yellow
Cosmos	*(C. bipinatus & C. sulphureus)*	multicolors
Engelmann daisy	*(Engelmannia pinnatifida)*	yellow
Evening primrose	*(Oenothera* spp.)	multicolors
Gayfeather	*(Liatris* spp.)	purple
Horsemint	*(Mondarda citriodora)*	lavender
Indian blanket	*(Gaillardia pulchella)*	red & yellow
Indian paintbrush	*(Castilleja indivisa)*	orange
Indian paintbrush	*(Castilleja purpurea)*	purple
Lemon mint	*(Monarda citriodora)*	purple
Maximillian sunflower	*(Helianthus maximiliani)*	yellow
Mexican hat	*(Ratibida columnaris)*	red & yellow
Ox-eyed daisy	*(Chrysanthemum leucanthemum)*	white
Purple coneflower	*(Echinacea purpurea)*	purple
Snow on the mountain	*(Euphorbia marginata)*	white
Tahoka daisy	*(Machaeranthera tanacetifolia)*	purple
White yarrow	*(Achillea millifolum)*	white
Gold yarrow	*(Achillea filipendulina)*	yellow

5
NATURAL ORGANIC PLANTING TECHNIQUES

DRAINAGE

Proper drainage isn't an option—it's a must. If a site doesn't drain, it won't work, and plants won't grow properly. Biological activity and proper nutrient exchange will be slowed or stopped—it's that simple. Drainage can be accomplished with surface and/or underground solutions. Any system that works is a good system. There are many organic products that will improve the physical structure and the drainage of any soil, but it's still a great benefit to start any project with proper grading and drainage techniques that will get rid of excess water as quickly as possible.

In residential and commercial projects, I recommend and use underground drain lines (perforated PVC pipe) set in gravel for hard-to-drain areas. Using pipe and gravel to drain tree holes can often be the difference between the success and the failure of newly planted plants. A ditch filled with gravel to the soil's surface is an excellent and inexpensive tool to drain water from a low spot. Use no filter fabric. It will clog up at some point and cause drainage problems.

Liquid biological products can also help improve drainage by stimulating the beneficial organisms in the soil. Aerated compost tea works well. Micronized products that contain mycorrhizal fungi are also excellent. Garrett Juice can also be helpful.

TREE PLANTING

Trees are the most important landscape element and the only element that actually increases property value. They are the structural features of the landscape and, besides being pleasing to look at and walk under, provide significant services such as blocking undesirable views, shading the ground and other plants, providing protection for wildlife, improving the soil, and providing delightful seasonal beauty.

It is for all these reasons that trees need to be planted correctly so that their root systems develop properly, providing a long, healthy life with a minimum of problems.

Here's how to plant trees organically—*the natural way*.

One of the most important points in this book is applicable anywhere in the country—the world actually—and that is how to plant trees properly. Almost all trees these days are being planted poorly, and the most serious infraction is planting too deep. When the top of the root ball and the root flare are buried in the ground, circling and girdling roots are hidden and many trees today are blowing over as a result. Even if that never happens, when soil is too high on the trunks of trees, the covered bark tissue stays moist all the time, and plant growth is dramatically slowed or even stopped. Trees that are too deep can be uncovered with the Air Spade or by hand, but the best solution is to plant trees correctly in the first place. You will notice that I also do not recommend staking, wrapping trunks, or using other unnecessary and damaging techniques.

Here are the details:

1. Dig an Ugly Hole
The hole should be dug slightly less shallow than the same depth as the height of the ball. Do not guess—actually measure the height of the ball. Never plant trees in slick-sided or glazed holes such as those caused by a tree spade or auger, unless the slick sides are destroyed at planting. Holes with glazed sides greatly restrict root penetration into the surrounding soil, can cause circling roots and consequently limit proper root development.

2. Run a Perk Test
Simply fill the hole with water and wait until the next day. If the water level does not drain away overnight, a drainage problem is indicated. At this point, the tree needs to be moved to another location or have drainage added in the form of a PVC drain line set in gravel running from the hole to a lower point on the site. Another draining method that sometimes works is a pier hole dug down from the bottom of the hole into a different soil type and filled with gravel. A sump from the top of the ball down to the bottom of the ball does little if any good. Positive drainage is critical, so do not shortcut this step. Spraying the sides of the holes with Garrett Juice or hydrogen peroxide will help initial root establishment.

3. Plant High
Most trees are planted too deep in the ground. The root flare is part of the trunk and should be placed above ground. Remove burlap, excess

soil, and mulch from the surface to expose the true top of the root ball. The top of the root ball should be slightly higher than ground grade.

When planting balled and burlapped plants, it's okay to leave burlap on the sides of the ball after planting, but loosen at the trunk and remove the burlap from the top of the ball. Remove any nylon or plastic covering or string, since these materials do not decompose and can girdle the trunk and roots as the plant grows. Studies have shown that even wire mesh should be removed to avoid root girdling because wire does not break down very fast.

When planting from plastic containers, carefully remove plants and tear the outside roots if they have grown solidly against the container. Never leave plants in containers. Bare-rooted, balled and burlapped, as well as container plant materials should be planted the same way. When planting bare-rooted plants, it is critical to keep the roots moist during the transportation and planting process.

4. Backfill with Existing Soil

Remove the excess soil from the top of the root ball and remove the "bird's nest" and/or circling roots. Place the tree in the center of the hole, making sure that the top of the ball is slightly higher than the sur-rounding grade. Backfill with the soil that was removed from the hole. This is a critical point. Do not add sand, foreign soil, organic material, or fertilizer into the backfill. The roots need to start growing in the native soil from the beginning. When the hole is dug in solid rock, topsoil from the same area should be used. Some native rock mixed into the backfill is beneficial. Adding amendments such as peat moss, sand, or foreign soils to the backfill not only wastes money, but is detrimental to the tree. Putting gravel in the bottom of the hole is a total waste of money.

5. Settle Soil with Water

Water the backfill thoroughly, making sure to get rid of all air pockets. Do not tamp the soil or air pockets will be formed and roots will be killed in these spots. Settle the soil with water only.

6. Do Not Wrap or Stake

Trunks of newly planted trees should not be wrapped. It is a waste of money, looks unattractive, harbors insects, and leaves the bark weak when removed. Tree wrapping is similar to a bandage left on your finger too long. If you are worried about the unlikely possibility of sunburn, it is much better to paint the trunk with a diluted latex paint that matches the color of the bark. White is OK too. Staking and guying is usually unnecessary if the tree has been planted properly with the proper earth ball size of at least nine inches of ball for each one inch of trunk diameter. Staking is a waste of money and detrimental to the proper trunk development of the plant. In rare circumstances (sandy soil, tall evergreen trees, etc.) where the tree needs to be staked for a while, connect the guy wires as low on the trunk as possible and remove the stakes as soon as possible. Never leave them on more than one growing season. Temporary staking should be done with strong wire and metal eyebolts screwed into the trunk. Staking should only be done as a last resort—it is unsightly, expensive, adds to mowing and trimming costs, and restricts the tree's ability to develop tensile strength in the trunk and trunk diameter. It can also cause damage to the cambium layer. Remove all tags.

7. Do Not Prune
It is very bad advice to prune at planting to compensate for the loss of roots during transplanting or planting. Most trees fare much better if all the limbs and foliage are left intact. The more foliage, the more food can be produced to build the root system. Even low limbs and foliage should be left on the tree for at least two growing seasons to aid root and trunk development. The health of the root system is the key to the overall health of the tree. The only trees that seem to respond positively to thinning at the time of transplanting are field-collected live oak, yaupon holly, and a few other evergreens. Plants purchased in containers definitely need no pruning, and deciduous trees never need to be thinned.

8. Mulch the Top of Ball
Mulch the top of the ball after planting with one inch of compost and then three inches of mulch tapering to zero inches at the tree trunk. This step is important in lawn areas or in beds. Do not ever plant grass over the tree ball until the tree is established. Do not build soil dykes for water. They are unsightly, unnecessary, and create a maintenance problem.

People don't grow trees. Trees grow in spite of people. For the most part, trees are tough, durable, and easy to plant and transplant if treated in a sensible and natural way.

Tree Planting Detail

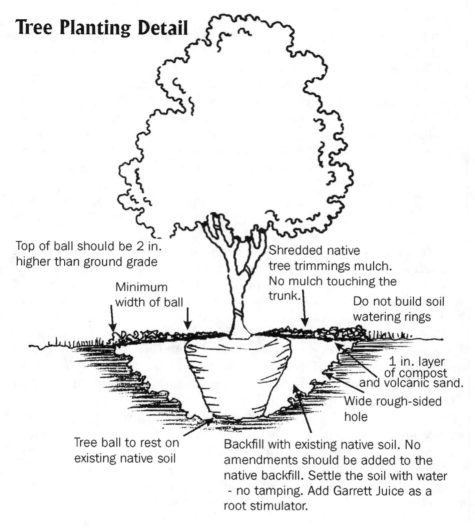

Top of ball should be 2 in. higher than ground grade

Minimum width of ball

Shredded native tree trimmings mulch. No mulch touching the trunk.

Do not build soil watering rings

1 in. layer of compost and volcanic sand.

Wide rough-sided hole

Tree ball to rest on existing native soil

Backfill with existing native soil. No amendments should be added to the native backfill. Settle the soil with water - no tamping. Add Garrett Juice as a root stimulator.

After backfilling:
- Add volcanic rock dust product to disturbed area at 10 lbs. per 1,000 sq. ft.
- Add 1″ compost and volcanic sand
- Add shredded tree trimmings mulch as shown. Do not pile mulch on trunks
- Do not stake trees
- Do not wrap tree trunks
- Do not thin or top trees
- Do not build watering rings

Note: Remove any soil that has been added to the top of root balls before planting. Remove the burlap from the top of ball and burlapped plants. Remove circling and girdling roots from all. Expose the actual top of the root ball.

LAWN PLANTING

Lawn planting techniques can be quite simple and economical, or complicated and wasteful. If you follow these simple techniques, your lawn establishment can be successful and affordable.

Soil preparation should include the hand or mechanical removal of all weeds, debris, and rocks more than two inches in diameter from the surface of the soil. Rocks within the soil are no problem because they can actually aid drainage. Herbicides are unnecessary and not recommended. Products like RoundUp are toxic and should not be used.

Lightly till or scarify the topsoil to a depth of two inches, rake smooth, and gently slope to prevent ponding of water. Deep rototilling is unnecessary and a waste of money unless the soil is heavily compacted. In fact, rototilling can actually damage the soil, especially if there are trees on the site.

Although the introduction of some organic material can be beneficial, soil amendments in general are unnecessary and only on solid rock areas is the addition of native topsoil needed. Imported foreign topsoil is a waste of money and can cause a perched (trapped) water table and lawn problem. Poor drainage is often a result of this procedure.

Prior to seeding, spray the soil with a biostimulant such as Garrett Juice and treat the seed with one of the same products. Apply a light application of organic fertilizer at the time of the first mowing. Good choices include compost, humate, and earthworms castings. Micronized products that contain mycorrhizal fungi are also very helpful.

Severely sloped areas should have an erosion protection material, such as jute mesh, placed on the soil prior to planting. Follow the manufacturer's recommendations for installation.

Some people still recommend and use toxic herbicides to kill weeds prior to planting. I don't! These chemicals are extremely hazardous and hard on the life in the soil. Use a little more elbow grease and dig the weeds out. The weeds' root system will actually help you establish the permanent grasses. Weeds can also be killed with vinegar or fatty acid products.

Seeding and hydromulching should be placed in direct contact with the soil. If hydromulching is used, the seed should be broadcast onto the bare soil first and then the hydromulch blown on top of the seed. One of the worse mistakes I see in grass planting is mixing the seed in the hydromulch. This causes the seed to germinate in the mulch, suspended above the soil, and many of the seeds are lost from drying out.

After spreading seed, thoroughly soak the seeded area as necessary to keep it moist. As the seed germinates, watch for bare spots. Reseed these bare areas immediately. Continue to use the light watering until the grass has solidly covered the area. At this time, begin the regular watering and maintenance program. Deep, infrequent waterings are best. Light watering done every day or every other day causes all kinds of problems, such as shallow roots, salt buildup in the top soil, and high water bills.

Solid sod blocks should be laid joint to joint after applying a liquid stimulant to the ground. Sod should be moistened on the bottom (soilside) before laying on moist ground. Grading, leveling, and smoothing prior to planting is important. Rolling with a heavy hand roller after planting is important to eliminate air pockets, which can cause brown spots in the sod. The joints between the blocks of sod can be filled with compost or granite sand to give a more finished look to the lawn, but this step is optional.

ORGANIC BED PREPARATION (GENERAL)

New Beds with no Grass or Existing Beds: No excavation is needed. Add four to six inches of compost, organic fertilizer (two pounds per hundred square feet), volcanic rock sand at four to ten pounds per hundred square feet and cornmeal and/or dry molasses at one to two pounds per hundred square feet, or ten to twenty pounds per thousand square feet, rototill or fork to a total overall depth of eight inches. Topdress bed with two-to-three-inch layer of shredded native-tree-trimmings mulch after planting.

New Beds in Grass Area: Remove existing sod with sod cutter or by hand to a depth of one and a half inches add four to six inches compost, organic fertilizer (two pounds per hundred square feet), volcanic rock powder at four pounds per hundred square feet and dry molasses at two pounds per hundred square feet, horticultural cornmeal at two pounds per hundred square feet, rototill to a total depth of eight inches. Top-dress beds with three-inch layer of shredded hardwood bark or native-tree-chip mulch after planting.

Azalea Bed Prep: Mix 50 percent shredded hardwood bark, cedar, or shredded coconut fiber and 50 percent finished compost. Add a five-gallon bucket of lava sand and a one-gallon bucket of greensand per cubic yard. Thoroughly moisten the mixture prior to placing in the bed. Excavate three inches and place fifteen inches of the above mix into the beds. The entire mixture can be put above ground if it doesn't block drainage. The top should be flat and the sides sloped at a 45 degree angle.

Note: Volcanic sand can be omitted if property has volcanic soil.

SHRUB, GROUND COVER, VINE, AND FLOWER PLANTING

Preparing landscape and garden beds correctly the first time allows the plants to establish more quickly, grow faster, and stay healthier. Many people get frustrated with the lack of results and either give up gardening or spend huge sums of money ripping out the plants, preparing the beds correctly, and replanting. So save some time, money, and aggravation by following these steps to begin with:

Remove Weeds and Grass: Excavate beds to a depth necessary to remove all weeds and grass, including rhizomes, one and a half to two inches deep is usually deep enough. Vinegar or fatty acid herbicides can be used, but do not use toxic chemical herbicides to kill grass and weeds. Never till the area first. This will drive the grasses into the soil to become serious weed problems forever.

Add Topsoil for Proper Grade: If needed, add native topsoil to all beds to within two inches of the adjacent finished grade. Avoid foreign unnatural materials, including soils that are different from the existing.

Add Compost: Cover areas to be planted with a four-to-six-inch depth of properly decomposed and composted organic material. In other words, use compost. Avoid the use of peat moss, raw barks, and other raw materials. Peat moss is okay if you live near a peat moss bog, but local or regionally made compost is better because it is alive.

Add Rock Minerals: Most soils have rock minerals, but, in most soils, the addition of granite sand, greensand, rock phosphate, lava sand, or other volcanic materials can be beneficial. Gypsum is good for soils deficient in sulfur and calcium.

Add Fertilizer: An application of an organic fertilizer should be broadcast at two pounds per hundred square feet or twenty pounds per thousand square feet onto the planting bed prior to tilling. An application of a biostimulant such as Garrett Juice is also beneficial. Fertilizers that contain mycorrhizal fungi are excellent to use.

Till Amendments Together with Native Soil: Till the amendments and the existing topsoil together until the amendments/soil mixture is eight to ten inches deep. Ground cover beds do not have to be tilled as deeply.

Never Till Wet Soil: Till, forking, or digging holes in wet soil does damage by squeezing the soil particles together, causing glazing and damage to the soil, eliminating the air spaces needed for good tilth and soil life.

Raise the Beds: The top of the beds should be flat and higher than sur-rounding grades with sloped edges for drainage. This lifting happens naturally if proper amounts of amendments are added to the new beds.

Moisten Beds before Planting: Planting beds should be moistened before the planting begins. Beds should be moist, but not sopping wet. Do not plant in dry soil because the young roots can become dehydrated quickly.

Tear Pot-Bound Roots: Pot-bound plants can resist water and cause the growth of deformed and unhealthy root systems. Cut or tear the mat of circling roots at the outside edge of the root ball, but don't destroy the root system.

Wet Roots into Moist Soil: Dip plant balls into water and install sopping wet roots into moist beds. Add compost tea or Garrett Juice to the water for best results. Mycorrhizal fungi products are also helpful.

Plant Level: Set the plants so that the top of the rootball is even or slightly higher than the surrounding soil. Setting the plant too low can cause drowning. Planting too high can cause the upper roots to dry out.

Mulch Beds after Planting: A two-to-three-inch layer of organic mulch should be placed on the soil after planting. Use shredded native tree trimmings for shrubs and ground cover and a thinner layer of compost for annuals and perennials. Do not pile mulch on the stems of plants.

Note: If it sounds simple, it is! Just add plenty of compost, rock minerals and molasses into the native soil and mulch all bare soil after planting.

PREPARATION OF FARM LAND

Agricultural land is handled much the same as the home vegetable gar-den or landscape. It's just that the size is greater, and it's more critical to be as efficient as possible with input costs. Let nature do as much of the work as possible.

Mechanical aeration and products with low cost per acre such as green manure cover crops, humates, molasses products, and other bio-logical stimulators are important tools.

Compost can also be an important tool for farm land. Less-than-fin-ished compost is best for agricultural fields. Compost that has only been turned one time is best so the completion of the composting process happens in or on the soil. Application should be done, if possible, six weeks prior to planting. Compost should be lightly tilled into the soil so that the escaping nitrogen is captured.

Aeration is critical. For tightly compacted soil, use a chisel plow or aerator to break through the hard pan. Use no-till or conservation tillage after the first year. Plowing should be avoided. Liquid products that can speed up the tilth improvement process include Garrett Juice, Nature's Creation, and Medina Plus. Application of dry or liquid molasses will also stimulate microorganisms and increase the natural fertility of the soil.

GARDENING BY THE MOON

People who garden by the moon believe that the same gravitational forces that move the tides up and down also have significant influence on plant growth. Most moon gardeners believe that the increasing light of the moon benefits those plants that bear fruit above the ground. Conversely, they believe that when the moon is on the wane, and its light and gravitational pull are on the decrease, the earth's gravity kicks in again and the plants that produce below the ground are benefited.

The *Old Farmer's Almanac* says that bulbs and vegetables that bear crops below ground should be planted during the dark of the moon. That is, from the day after it is full to the day before it is new again. Anything like radishes, onions, potatoes, etc. that grow underneath the ground will grow larger and produce better. If you plant on the new moon, they'll grow tall and bloom, but the underground veggies won't be good.

Planting should not be done when the moon is absolutely dark because that's when plants should rest. The new moon or dark of the moon seems to be a good time to prune and kill weeds because they won't grow back as readily.

Moon gardeners have different opinions, and you can hardly find two who plant exactly the same way. And they all think they're right, because whichever way they choose seems to work in general.

If you have the time to pay attention to cosmic forces as shown to us by the moon and stars, gardening by the moon can be fun and very productive.

MULCH CHOICES

Mulch is a critical ingredient in any organic program. It helps conserve moisture, buffers the soil from temperature extremes, shades out weeds, looks nice, and increases the tilth of the soil. It also supplies food for soil life and nutrients for the soil, keeps raindrops from compacting the soil, keeps the sun from burning the humus out of the soil, and prevents erosion.

After planting any kind of plant—tree, shrub, ground cover, flower, or vegetable, all bare soil should be covered with natural organic mulch. Mulch is not a soil amendment mixed into the soil—it's a covering placed on top of the finished planting bed after the plants have been installed.

Not all mulches are created equal. There are many acceptable mulches, but they vary in quality and effectiveness. One of the best top-dressing mulches is partially decomposed compost. I discovered the benefit of this material at home as a result of being too impatient to wait on my own compost pile to finish its decomposition. The not-quite-finished compost has larger particles and does a good job of mulching and letting oxygen breathe through to the soil surface but carbon dioxide escapes out to be captured by the mulch.

Grass clippings should only be used as a mulch if mixed with leaves and other debris. I don't recommend lawn grass clippings as a mulch by themselves because the flat blades plate and seal off the soil's gas exchange. Grass clippings should be left on the lawn.

Straw and hay can be used if they are free of broadleaf herbicide residue. Alfalfa is the best hay mulch because of its nutrient value and the presence of *tricontanol*, a growth regulator.

Another excellent mulch is shredded hardwood bark. It is tree bark that has been run through a hammer mill. This smashing action gives the bark its fibrous texture, which helps to hold it in place in your beds even on slopes, but still allows air to circulate down to the soil. A less expensive and even better material is shredded native tree trimmings. It looks good and works beautifully. An added benefit of the tree trimmings mulch is that the buds, leaves, and cambium layers contain protein, which provides nitrogen and other nutrients.

Not all bark makes a good top-dressing mulch. For example, the fine to medium grades of pine bark make, at best, a second-rate mulch. Pine bark consists of flat pieces that plate together and seal off the oxygen from the soil. Pine bark often washes or blows away. The tars and resins in pine bark can also inhibit proper aerobic degradation. The only pine bark that makes a decent mulch is the large, nugget size because it will at least stay in place well. The large nuggets don't fit together tightly, so air can still circulate around the pieces down to the soil, and large pieces don't rob nitrogen from the soil as fine-particle mulch sometimes does. However, in general, I am not a big pine bark fan. It's better than no mulch at all—but barely.

Pine needles are a good choice when used as a top-dressing mulch, especially when used in parts of the country where pine trees are growing. There's also an economic advantage when the material is locally available and can be gathered from the forest floor, although care should be taken not to deplete the organic matter in any natural setting.

Walnut should not be used as a mulch until fully composted. The raw material contains juglans which has strong growth-retarding properties.

Sawdust is sometimes used as a mulch, but I don't recommend it unless it has been mixed with coarser materials and composted for a while. Sawdust does make an excellent carbon ingredient for the compost pile.

Pecan shells make a fair top-dressing mulch, but are much better if composted first with other vegetative materials. Pecan shells are not good to mix into the soil.

Shredded cypress makes a lousy mulch. It tends to mat and seal off oxygen. It breaks down very slowly, and, contrary to popular opinion, that's a problem. It's an environmental problem to ship any mulch or compost material great distances. It's also an environmental problem to harvest cypress tress from coastal areas.

I do not recommend the artificial mulches such as plastic, rubber fabric, nor do I recommend gravel as a mulch. The non-organic mulches don't biodegrade and don't return anything to the soil. I also don't recommend dyed and colored mulches. Natural mulches of organic matter will eliminate most weeding and cultivation, eliminate soil compaction, save money on irrigation, preserve and stimulate the soil microorganisms and earthworms, and maintain the ideal soil temperature. In the heat of summer, the soil surface under a proper layer of mulch will be around 82-85°. The temperature of bare soil can be in excess of 120°.

Some alleged experts say that whenever a highly carbonaceous mulch such as bark mulch is used, decomposition organisms will steal nitrogen from the soil unless a fertilizer is added that supplies 1 lb. of nitrogen for each 100 lbs. of mulch. Not true! For years, I have mulched with hay, bark, tree chips, etc. without supplying extra nitrogen and have never observed any symptoms of nitrogen deficiency as long as the mulch stays on the top of the soil. When raw organic matter is tilled into the soil, there usually is nitrogen draft. Finished compost only should be tilled into the soil. People who still till peat moss and bark into the soil are behind the times.

Conclusion: use compost to prepare planting beds, and use a coarse-textured natural mulch on the surface of the soil after the plants have been installed.

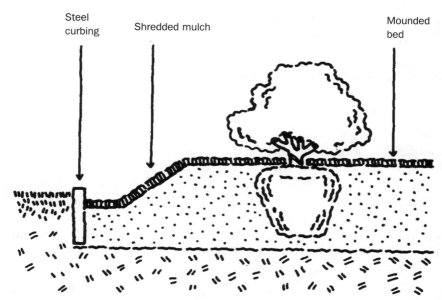

Mulches: To Be Used After Planting. Planting beds should be raised, sloped down on the edge, and covered with a thick blanket of mulch.

Your Basic Mulch Options

Compost: Compost is an excellent mulch for annuals and perennials and for use as a top-dressing mulch for newly planted young trees. A light layer of compost is also beneficial on new shrub and groundcover beds prior to the addition of the coarse mulch. Compost is magic! At least it contains nature's magic. It is also effective to use around sick trees and other plants to help them recover. Compost is nature's fertilizer. A thin layer of compost is the best choice for young seedlings of any kind.

Cypress Chips: Shredded cypress mulch is not good mulch and shouldn't be used. It's long lasting but that isn't a good thing. Mulch should break down relatively quickly to produce humus and organic acids to fee microorganisms. Harvest cypress from coastal areas is an environmental mistake.

Hardwood Bark: Shredded hardwood bark is an excellent mulch material for ornamental planting beds. It is fibrous and has coarse and fine particles, so it grows fungi quickly. The microbes lock the material together to prevent washing and blowing, but still allow air transfer to the soil. Hardwood mulch is one of the best choices to use around newly planted trees, shrubs, and other permanent plants. It's also good for potted plants.

Hay: Clean hay is good for vegetable gardens. Alfalfa is the best choice—Bermuda is the worst because of possible broadleaf herbicide contamination. Eight-to-ten-inch layers are needed to prevent weed seed germination.

Pine Bark: Pine bark is used widely as a bed preparation material, but shouldn't be. First of all, it won't stay in place and has a strong tendency to wash and blow away. Very fine particles of mulch can sometimes rob some of the nitrogen from the soil. The large size deco bark is a fair mulch to use for shrubs and ground covers. The large size of the deco bark allows air to flow around the large pieces and down to the soil and to the plants' roots. Fine and medium size pine bark is not a good mulch choice. As pine bark breaks down, some rather nasty natural chemicals are released.

Pine Needles: Pine needles are an excellent mulch to use in most planting beds, but they are certainly more appropriate when used in areas where pine trees grow, so they don't look out of place. Pine needles are a much better choice than pine bark.

Shredded Native Tree Trimmings: This nulch is good to use in large areas as a natural ground cover. If ground into smaller texture, this mulch can be used on all types of plants. Because of the buds and cambium layer under the bark, this mulch contains more nitrogen than most mulches and, therefore, doesn't take any nitrogen from the soil. Shredded trees and shrubs from your own property are my favorite of all mulches. This material, when partially composted or mixed with compost, is the very best mulch of all. These mulches are known as "living mulches".

"Mulching by itself cannot make up for the shortfall of fertility in the soil"
—Dr. William A. Albrecht

"But it can certainly take you in the right direction."
—Howard Garrett

Organic Mulches

Organic Mulches	Rating	Application	Remarks
Pine bark (large size)	Fair	3" deep in ornamental beds.	Works well but some people don't like the look.
Pine bark (small to medium)	Bad	Use as a last resort only.	Washes and blows around. Flat pieces tend to seal off oxygen from the soil.
Cedar	Excellent	Shredded cedar is one of the best mulches.	Deoiled cedar flakes are the very best greenhouse flooring material.
Coffee grounds	Poor	Best to use in compost pile.	Slightly acid. Will blow and wash away.
Compost	Excellent	Use partially decomposed material 3–5" thick.	Save the more decomposed to till directly in the soil.
Corncobs (ground)	Fair	Apply 3" thick.	Availability may be a problem.
Cornstalks (chopped)	Fair	Apply 4–6" deep in vegetable gardens.	Very coarse texture.
Cottonseed hulls	Fair	Apply 3–4" deep.	Have fertilizer value similar to cottonseed meal. Very light and tend to blow around.
Cypress chips	Poor	Don't use.	Can seal off oxygen. Harvest is an environmental problem.
Lawn clippings	Poor	Better left on the lawn or mixed into compost pile.	Good source of nitrogen. Flat pieces plate and seal off oxygen.
Leaves	Good	Best run through a chipper before applying 3" deep.	Blowing and washing can be a problem.
Manure	Fair	Apply only after composting.	Fresh manure can burn plants and can contain weed seeds.

Organic Mulches, Continued

Organic Mulches	Rating	Application	Remarks
Pecan shells, Peanut shells, Rice hulls	Good	Apply 3" deep. Better to compost first with other materials.	Inexpensive, becoming more available, high in nitrogen.
Peat moss	Terrible	Don't use; the worst mulch choice.	Expensive, blows and washes away.
Pine needles	Excellent	Apply 3–5" thick on vegetable gardens and ornamental beds.	Looks best when used in association with pine trees.
Sawdust	Poor	Use in the compost pile, not as a mulch.	Small pieces seal off oxygen exchange when used as a mulch.
Seaweed	Fair	Not readily available but works well.	Watch for salt content. Decomposes slowly.
Straw, hay	Good	Apply 4–5" deep in ornamental beds, 8–10" deep in vegetable garden.	Use for winter protection. Alfalfa is the best. Bermuda grass is the worst because of possible chemical contamination.
Shredded hardwood bark	Excellent	Apply 3–4" deep in ornamental beds.	Best mulch of all for use on sloped areas.
Shredded native tree trimmings	Excellent	Apply 3–4" deep in ornamental beds.	Even better when mixed with compost.
Gravel	Poor	Best used at 3–6" in utility areas.	Large, decorative stones are good for use in shady landcape areas.
Lava rock	Fair	Apply 3–5" deep	Avoid using in large areas— too harsh.
Shredded native Cedar	Excellent	Apply 3-4" deep around all plantings	Use a thinner layer around vegetables, small flowers, and native plants that have low water requirements.

NATURAL ORGANIC MAINTENANCE

Working With Nature's Systems

NATURAL TREE CARE

Pruning: Is it time to thin my trees and cut off the lower limbs? My answers to these common questions might surprise you. There seems to be an abundance of curious tree-pruning advice still around. Let's try to straighten it out.

Pruning too much is the most common mistake. Few trees need major pruning every year. Other than some fruit trees, few trees need annual thinning and, unless lower limbs are a physical problem, they should be left on the tree.

Timing: Landscape trees can be pruned any time of the year, but the best time is from fall to late winter. Fruit trees should be pruned from midwinter up until bud break. Certain fruit trees like peach trees, should only be pruned just before bud break because pruning induces bud break and flowering. Early flowers and late freezes spell no fruit.

Amount of Pruning: Pruning trees is part science and part art. Don't try to change the character and overall, long-term shape of a tree, and don't remove lower limbs to raise the canopy. Low growing limbs exist for a reason. It's very unnatural to strip tree trunks bare. If you think that looks good, think again. Remove dead, diseased, broken, or damaged limbs and the weakest of crossing limbs. Remove limbs that grow toward the center of the tree and limbs that are dangerous or physically interfere with buildings or activities. Thinning to eliminate a certain percentage of the foliage is usually a mistake. Heavy thinning of a tree's canopy throws the plant out of balance, inviting wind and ice storm damage. The resulting stress attracts diseases and insect pests. Gutting (heavy interior pruning) is never appropriate.

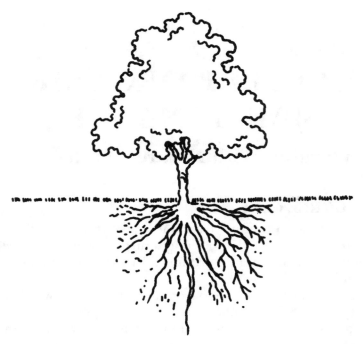

How people think tree roots grow. ·

How tree roots really grow.

Pruning Cuts: Pruning cuts should be made with sharp tools. Hand tools such as bow saws, Japanese pruning saws, loppers, and pole pruners are good for small limbs. Chain saws can be used for larger limbs, but only with great care and a thorough understanding of the equipment.

Flush cuts should never be made. Cuts leaving a one-sixteenth-inch stub are also bad. Pruning cuts should be made at the point where the branch meets the trunk, just outside the branch collar. The branch collar stub will be as small as one-eighth or one-fourth inch on small limbs, but can extend from several inches to as much as a foot or more on large limbs. It will also be wider at the bottom of the limb than at the top. Cuts made at the right place leave a round wound. Improper flush cuts leave oval wounds and cause cavities to form in the trunk long term.

It's scientific fact that cutting into or removing the branch collar causes problems. Flush cuts encourage decay. They also destroy the natural protective zone between the trunk and the branch and can cause several serious tree problems including discolored wood, decayed wood, wet wood, resin pockets, cracks, sun injury, cankers, and slowed growth of new wood. Proper cuts are round, smaller, and heal much faster. Peach, plum, apricot, and other fruit trees are particularly sensitive to flush cuts. Many fruit tree insects and disease problems are related to improper pruning cuts. Long branch stubs can also be detrimental sometimes and should be avoided. However, it is always better to err on the side of stubs too long than too short.

Wound Dressings: Research by Alex Shigo, Carl Whitcomb, and the U.S. Forest Service has shown that pruning paint and wound dressings have no benefit and can be harmful by slowing the healing process. Healthy tissue needed for callus formation can be damaged or killed by pruning paint or dressings. Trees have defense cells, much like white blood cells in mammals. These lignin cells are produced on the backside of a wound to naturally prevent diseases from entering fresh cuts. Just as a cut finger heals faster when exposed to the air, so does a tree wound.

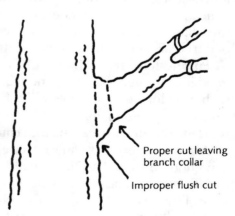

Proper cut leaving branch collar

Improper flush cut

Cavities: Cavities are often caused by flush cuts. Cavities in trees are voids where fungi have rotted healthy material. They are usually the result of physical injury. Removing only the decayed material is the remedy. Fillers such as concrete and foam are only cosmetic and are not recommended. When removing decayed matter from cavities, be careful not to cut or punch into the healthy tissue. Injuries to healthy tissue can introduce further decay into the tree. When cavities hold water, drain tubes are sometimes inserted to release water. Bad idea. Drain tubes puncture the protective barriers between the rotted and healthy wood and allow decay to expand. I don't recommend any of the trunk injector systems for fertilizer and insect control because of their puncture wounds—plus they miss the main problem of improving the health of the soil.

Cabling: Weak crotches between limbs can sometimes be stopped from splitting by installing cables horizontal to the ground so the natural movement of the tree is not completely stopped. Cabling used to hold up low growing limbs is poor tree care and a waste of money. Cabling can be very dangerous and should only be done by professional arborists. In most cases, I do not recommend it.

As a final note, the tree trimmings and sawdust resulting from pruning should not be hauled away. The large pieces should be used for firewood and the limbs and foliage should be shredded and used as mulch under trees or mixed into a compost pile.

Fertilizing: Since all plants require food, trees should not be overlooked when a landscape is fertilized. The easiest way to fertilize trees is in conjunction with the general fertilization of the grass and planting beds beneath the trees. The feeder roots are near the surface, and the tree will use whatever nutrients are there. Remember that more than 80 percent of a tree's root system is in the top twelve to eighteen inches of soil.

Putting fertilizer in holes drilled throughout the root zone is not a good idea for general fertilization, but is effective for a specific deficiency such as chlorosis. The roots will take the concentrated material (sulfur, iron, or magnesium, for example) from the cores as needed. What's better is to feed the entire root zone with compost and quality organic fertilizers.

A good balanced, organic fertilizer is perfect for establishing a healthy condition for trees. Fertilizer should be applied two or three times a year, as with other plantings. Placing a layer of compost over the entire root zone of the tree (and beyond) will help greatly to feed the soil and thus the tree. Healthy plants will repel insects and diseases, reducing or eliminating the need for pest control products. Periodic applications of foliar food are also beneficial. The best foliar feeding products are aerated compost tea, Garrett Juice, and mycorrihizal fungi products.

Aeration: Mechanical hole punching of the soil is recommended for sick trees, especially in clay or other heavy soils. Oxygen is one of the most important elements in healthy soil. Air penetration helps greatly to stimulate microbial activity and root growth. Physical aeration help is only needed in the first year of any organic program. Healthy soil will have natural aeration.

Pest Control: Occasionally, trees need to be sprayed to control certain pests or to give them a little extra nutrient punch. In an organic program, this can be accomplished in one step, reducing the cost once again. Garrett Juice and aerated compost tea are again the best tools. Foliar feeding will indirectly help control most harmful insects without killing the beneficial ones. At the same time, the sprays provide nutrients for the tree. Foliar feeding helps with pest control by improving the immune system of the plants and by feeding and stimulating beneficial microorganisms. When orange oil or d-limonene is added at two ounces per gallon of spray, the spray actually kills pests. It will also kill beneficials, so use sparingly. See appendix for formula.

One of the most persistent pests is the aphid, which is the most prevalent in the spring when trees start their active growth cycle. Aphids damage plants by sucking the juices from tender, new growth. There is a very easy way to control aphids—spray with garlic/pepper tea, or molasses and orange oil at two ounces per gallon of water. A water blast followed by the release of ladybugs is my favorite aphid control because it doesn't hurt the beneficials.

Protecting and adding to the beneficial insect population will give effective control of aphids and other harmful insects. Good insects include ground beetles, spiders, ladybugs, green lacewings, praying mantids, wasps, and mud daubers, but there are many more.

Taking care of trees using common-sense techniques and safe products is easy and cost effective. The results are better than using toxic chemical treatments, which will destroy many beneficial insects while only reducing a percentage of the target pest insects. Imagine being able to spray trees without worrying about wind drift, lawsuits, over-application of material, and the real possibility that the environment is being harmed each time a pesticide is applied. That's the beauty of tree care using the natural approach—it is safer and it works better—in every way!

LAWN CARE

Grass is the most intensely maintained of all plants and the biggest expense in most landscape maintenance budgets. It is scalped, mowed, fertilized, sprayed before weeds appear, sprayed after weeds appear, walked on, driven on, and usually abused all during the year. As with all plant types, there are some cost effective, organic approaches for the natural care of grasses.

Mowing: Many turf areas are mowed too low. When grass is mowed short, the root system is correspondingly too short. That increases the demand for water and food, encourages weeds to germinate, and can cause the lawn to decline.

Generally, turf should be mowed to a height of at least two and a half inches or taller and should not be allowed to grow taller than one-thrid of its height between mowing. Cutting more than one-third of the grass blades can cause noticeable damage to the grass, which can take several days to overcome. Golf courses and other playing field turf areas don't always have the luxury of letting the grass grow taller but landscape areas certainly do.

Another important mowing technique is to leave the grass clippings on the ground. Don't bag them and haul them away—a practice that wastes time and money and is detrimental to the lawn. There's also an environmental issue related to the crowded condition of municipal land-fills. Grass clippings in plastic bags have been responsible for a large per-centage of the waste in city dumps.

Grass clippings left on the lawn will decompose rapidly in the presence of water and organic fertilizer, creating food for microbes and the resulting humus in the soil. Since the organic matter makes the soil healthier, the number of weeds will be reduced. Discarding the grass clippings also throws nutrients away. Tests at the University of Connecti-

cut agricultural experiment station showed, through the use of radioactive isotopes, that nitrogen in grass clippings left on the lawn was back in the growing plants in as short a time as one week.

Scalping a lawn in the spring is a waste of time and money. It is also harmful to the lawn. When the soil is exposed through scalping, humus is burned out of the soil, microbes suffer, and weed seed germinate.

Aeration: Aerating the soil is an important procedure in establishing soil health and going "organic." Soil will naturally become aerated by the addition of humus and the stimulation of earthworms and microbial activity if given enough time. All you have to do is add compost and organic fertilizers and stop using harsh, synthetic products, and nature will take over.

However, most of us want the process to go faster, and the answer is "punching holes" in the ground. These holes can be punched with a stiff-tined turning fork or any spiked tool. The most convenient method is to buy or rent an aerator or hire a landscape contractor to use a mechanical aerator to poke holes all over the yard.

Mechanical aerators are available in all shapes and sizes with many features. Some just punch small holes, others remove cores, and some inject water while punching holes. Some can even punch holes twelve inches deep. All these machines work. The more holes, the better, and the deeper the holes, the better. Just choose a machine that fits your budget, because the cost ranges greatly. The object is getting oxygen into the soil. When that happens, microbe populations start to increase instantly, natural nitrogen cycles function properly, and nature's wonderful systems are set in motion, It's not necessary to understand all the systems in great detail—it's only important to respect their presence and let them work for you.

Fertilizing Lawns: Another tip for good organic lawn care is to avoid synthetic chemical fertilizers, which are usually applied three, four, or more times a year. They green up a lawn quickly, but their effect soon falls off as the chemicals are leached out of the soil or washed down the street. Besides, they create a major hardship for the poor guy who's pushing the mower because chemical fertilizers create flushes of heavy growth. Synthetic fertilizers feed the plants artificially, too fast and do nothing for the soil, so their long-term effect is quite damaging.

Organic fertilizers provide the proper nutrients without damaging the soil. Natural fertilizers only need to be applied two or three times a year, are safe, and don't leach away. They release nutrients slowly, feeding the plants only what's needed and at the proper time. The result is green, healthy grass with slower, more consistent growth, making it easier to avoid having to catch the grass clippings.

Supplemental feeding of a lawn can be done at any time using liquid foliar sprays such as aerated compost tea and Garrett Juice. Foliar feeding will prevent the chlorotic look that lawns often have in late summer when the hot, dry days take their toll. It can also be used on grass areas any time to give the color a boost. Foliar feeding can reduce stress damage and improve cold tolerance. Liquid seaweed is an important ingredient in any spray program. Garrett Juice contains seaweed.

Spreader Settings: Most broadcast spreaders, set fully open, will dispense this fertilizer at approximately ten pounds per thousand square feet per pass. A crisscoss application usually gives the recommend twenty pounds.

Pest Control: The next lawn care necessity is spraying for all the things that don't belong. Most of the harmful insects, fungi, and bacteria can be controlled with beneficial nematodes and food products such as garlic and cornmeal. Plant Wash is an excellent commercial product. A healthy soil that drains well is the best long-term control.

Weeds can be controlled with organic products. Building a healthy soil, applying adequate organic fertilizer and water, and mowing on time will prevent most weeds, but there are no nontoxic herbicides on the market today that are foolproof. The only foolproof method of safely eliminating weeds is hand pulling or mechanical devices. Organic herbicide can be made by mixing one teaspoon of soap, one ounce of orange oil, and one tablespoon of molasses into one gallon of 10 percent white vinegar.

Composting Lawns: Composting helps both in fertilization and weed control. A one-quarter to one-inch layer of compost spread over a lawn once a year will provide the grass most of the nutrients it needs. It is an expensive process compared to cheap chemical fertilizers, but it improves the health of the soil and grass and will act as a buffer to extreme climatic changes and even to harsh chemicals. When funds are limited, composting every other year will usually be adequate. This process isn't needed any longer once the soil is healthy.

Compost will also help prevent weeds by increasing the health of the soil. Few noxious weeds will grow in a healthy, balanced soil, and the few that do appear are easily removed by hand or spot spraying. Learning to accept a lawn with a mix of grasses, wildflowers, and herbs is not only okay but recommended. We call that "multi-species" turf.

Safe lawn care is critical because the lawn is where the most people-use occurs, and the absence of chemicals means a healthier environment for children, pets, and others. Children are a very special concern, but the elderly and ill people of all ages are also particularly sensitive.

Renovating a Worn-Out Lawn: For compacted, weedy, unhealthy lawn areas: first mechanically aerate and don't be bashful—tear up the ground. Next, spray the area with Garrett Juice. Next, apply an organic fertilizer at twenty pounds per thousand square feet. For additional help, add one-fourth inch of compost, which is about 1 cubic yard per 1,300 sq. ft.

SHRUB, GROUND COVER, VINE, AND FLOWER CARE

Shrubs, ground covers, flowers, and vines are the easiest plants to maintain. Sometimes they need light pruning, fertilizing and even spraying, but they are easily accessible (unlike trees), and do not require intense maintenance unlike grass.

Pruning: Pruning shrubs, ground covers, and perennial flowers is really quite simple. Only remove enough growth to keep the plants under control. For example, most ground covers will need to be pruned back once in the early spring to remove the dead stubble and after that only when they encroach on paved surfaces or other planting areas. Ground covers and vines should be removed from the trunks and bases of trees every winter.

Perennials should be pruned in the late fall or winter to remove the previous year's dead growth. Or prune in the season opposite the bloom period. For example, prune spring-blooming perennials in the fall and fall-blooming perennials in the spring. Additional heavy pruning after strong flushes of flowers have started to play out will often promote a new flush of flowers.

Shrubs need more frequent pruning to keep them under control. Light, selective pruning is the best technique. Never prune shrubs by removing a large amount of growth or by constantly "boxing" them, which removes all the new growth. Not only does it make the shrub look artificial, it will ultimately ruin the usefulness of the plant and weaken it by reducing the photosynthetic surface. The exception here, of course, is a formal garden, which does require clipped hedges.

Fertilizing: As with trees and lawns, landscape beds should be fed with organic fertilizers two or three times a year. Flowers will usually need supplemental fertilizers like Garrett Juice, fish meal, or organic fertilizers. Micronized products are also helpful.

Pest Control: As a general rule, spraying to kill insects is not necessary and should not be done on a calendar or preventative basis, but, instead, at the first sign of infestation. For example, the annual ritual of applying insecticides in August for grubworms is one of the most blatant wastes of money and sources of pollution in landscape maintenance. Grubs are only damaging enough to treat when eight to ten per square foot are found. Most grub worms are actually beneficial. Work to improve the soil through aeration and organic fertilizers. Dry molasses and beneficial nematodes will eliminate heavy infestations.

Composting: Compost should be used around shrubs, ground covers, and flowers to help increase soil health, moisture retention, climate buffering, and weed control. Whenever compost is used as a mulch, it should be spread approximately one and a half to two inches deep. Once the ground is covered with plant growth, a light (one-half inch) application of compost is plenty.

Interior Plants: Interior plants should be planted in well-drained, organic potting soil. My favorites are mixes of compost, coconut fiber, and expanded shale. Soil Mender makes my specific formula. Potting soil should not be sterile, but alive with microorganisms and earthworms. Some of the best fertilizers for interior plants include earthworm castings, kelp meal, and coffee grounds. They are mild and odor free. Volcanic rock such as lava sand should also be added to the potting soils. Nature's Creation has Quick Dissolve Tables that are excellent for interior plants.

Pests on interior plants are best controlled by using liquid seaweed, Neem, garlic tea, and biostimulants. Orange oil products can be used for severe problems. Plant Wash is one of the best products for both insect and disease issues.

For success, give your interior plants plenty of light, moderate amounts of water and fertilization, and a gentle misting of water

regularly. If your water is alkaline, add one tablespoon of apple cider vinegar to each gallon of water.

Organic maintenance in general is really just a matter of copying what Nature does when left alone—it allows only adaptable plants to survive, strives to keep the ground covered, and utilizes organic matter in a never-ending cycle. Man has disrupted that cycle over the years, but, by using common sense and natural organic products, the balance can be re-established. Patterning any landscape maintenance program after Nature's own cycles will go a long way toward repairing the damage that has been done. You will grow more beautiful plants than ever imagined.

BASIC ANIMAL ORGANIC PROGRAM
Cooking for Your Pet

Healthy Pet Diet for Dogs
50% grain (rice, barley, etc.)
25% meat (rabbit, chicken, etc.)
25% veggies (steamed)
2% natural diatomaceous earth
1/8 tsp. Food grade kelp (daily)

Healthy Pet Diet for Cats
50% meat
25% grain
25% veggies (steamed)
2% natural diatomaceous earth
1/8 tsp. Food grade kelp (daily)

If you don't like to cook for your pets, buy and feed dogs and cats Muenster Natural Pet Foods. For information call 800-772-7178.

Pet Food Additives: For extra help in fighting fleas and internal parasites, give animals natural diatomaceous earth at 2 percent of the volume of food and The Missing Link. For information call 800-615-0031. Add a teaspoon of apple cider vinegar to your pet's water. Don't forget to brush, bathe, and exercise your pets regularly!

MAKING COMPOST

Compost is a living fertilizer that can be made at home or purchased ready to use. A compost pile can be started at any time of the year. Anything once alive can and should be composted. Good ingredients include leaves, hay, grass clippings, tree trimmings, food scraps, dead animals, bark, sawdust, rice hulls, weeds, spoiled food, nut hulls, animal manure, and anything else that was once alive. Mix the ingredients together in a container of wood, hay bales, hog wire, or concrete blocks or simply pile the material on the ground. Unless space is limited, free standing piles are preferred.

The ideal mixture is 80 percent vegetative matter and 20 percent animal waste, although any mix will compost. The ingredients should be basically a mix of coarse and fine-textured material. Avoid having all the pieces of material the same size. Large particles help aerate the pile and smaller pieces are needed to help hold moister and protect microbes.

Try to turn the pile at least once a month; oxygen speeds up the process. Keep the pile moist, roughly the moisture of a squeezed-out sponge, to help the living microorganisms thrive and work their magic. If you never turn the pile, it will still compost—it will just be slower.

Compost is ready to use when the ingredients are no longer identifiable. The color will be dark brown, the texture soft and crumbly, and the aroma that of a forest floor. Use compost in all bed preparation and as a high-quality mulch around annuals and perennials.

Compost location: Anywhere, sun or shade, on soil or on concrete.

Compost ingredients: Anything that was once alive.

Compost balance: To encourage a higher percentage of fungal activity compared with bacterial activity, add rock phosphate and keep the pile drier.

Compost Tea: Foliar feeding and soil drenching liquid made by soaking compost in water. If the compost tea is aerated, it has considerable greater quality.

Making Aerated Compost Tea

To make quality compost tea, start with good fungus-filled compost that contains aerobic beneficial microbes, then make them multiply by feeding and aerating them with a simple aquarium pump to increase the number of microbes including bacteria, fungi, protozoa, flagellates, and beneficial nematodes. Typical garden soils are weakest in fungal species, and this procedure helps them greatly. Buy a pump rated for about a fifty-gallon aquarium. Do not overdo the movement of tea and beat your fungus to death, but provide enough oxygen to keep the tea from going anaerobic.

Air stones, also from the pet store, are used to pump air through the tea by creating lots of bubbles. When stones become stained from the tea, clean them between each batch of tea by soaking them in a hydrogen peroxide (3 percent solution that comes from the grocery store). Cleaning the tea maker between every tea batch is also very important.

Worm castings are one of the best composts for making tea, but any quality compost will work. Compost can be put in a nylon tea bag or loose. Larger air stones go on the bottom of the bucket. Small air stones can be put in the tea bag. Five gallon buckets are good to use and will make about four gallons of tea. Add one-half ounce of molasses per gallon of water to help feed the microbes. Too much molasses can destroy microbes in the tea. Look at the movement of the water to make sure you have plenty of air and water movement. Put a lid on the bucket and let the tea brew for six or eight hours.

Molasses will give the tea a sweet smell. When the molasses is used up, the aroma of the tea will change to a yeasty aroma. Remove the tea bags if used and continue to brew the tea with the air pump running for another sixteen to twenty hours. The tea will start to deteriorate immediately after the air pump is turned off. You can prolong the life of the tea for a day by leaving the air on, but, when all the food has been used up, it will deteriorate even with the air on. Never try to store your finished tea in a closed container. It will develop pressure inside and blow.

Five gallons of tea will cover an acre of planting. As a soil drench five gallons will cover about ten thousand square feet of lawn or garden. It doesn't matter how much water you use to dilute and spread the tea. Bruce Lee Dueley has an even more thorough explanation of this process on his website: www.deuleysown.com. Also visit Captain Compost's website: www.captaincompostalabama.com. He is also the compost moderator in the forums of www.dirtdoctor.com.

The commercial alternative to compost brewing is extraction. No aeration is needed for this product and it has a shelf life of five to ten days. The easiest alternative is to use Nature's Creation micronized compost product, which can be mixed with water and sprayed as needed.

MONTHLY NATURAL ORGANIC MAINTENANCE CALENDAR

JANUARY

Plant*:
- Cold hardy transplants outdoors during mild weather. If you'd like to roll the dice on the future weather, try cabbage, calendulas, dianthus, flowering kale, pansies, snapdragons.
- Spring flowers and vegetable seeds indoors.
- Seeds in greenhouse conditions for later transplanting.
- Fruit and pecan trees, anemones, asparagus, berries, English peas, grapes, onions, potatoes, and ranunculus.
- Shrubs, vines, trees and other permanent plants.
- Complete tulip, daffodil and other bulb plantings in early January. "Force" bulbs in pots indoors. Paperwhites are the easiest to grow and smell terrific.
- Transplant plants during this dormant period.

Fertilize:
- Drench Garrett Juice as a root stimulator for new shrubs and trees monthly until established.
- Asparagus beds in late January with manure-based organic fertilizer and compost.
- Cool season grasses at one-half rate, about ten pounds per thousand square feet.
- Apply greensand to any plants that appeared chlorotic (yellow leaves with green veins) at about eighty pounds per thousand square feet.

Prune:
- Remove all vines from trees and pull groundcovers back from the bases of trees.
- Shade trees by removing dead, damaged and out of place limbs, water sprouts and ground shoots.
- Do not routinely "thin" trees unless more light is needed for understory plants.
- Summer-flowering trees as necessary to control form.
- DO NOT prune the tops of crape myrtles. The seed pods are decorative and some bird species like the seeds.
- Evergreen shrubs lightly if needed.
- Fruit trees and grapes. However, the best time is just before bud break as late in winter as possible.
- Do not make flush cuts, protect the branch collars, and do not use pruning paint. Do not overprune any wood plants, other than large perennials such as butterfly bush.

Water:
- Spot water any dry areas to avoid plant desiccation.
- Potted plants.
- Entire properties during drought periods.

Pest Control:
- WEEDS: Spray dormant turf with vinegar-based herbicide for cool season weeds. Do not use the so-called vinegars made from 99 percent acetic acid. Use real 10 percent vinegar made from grain alcohol.
- INSECTS: Horticultural oil if needed on scale-prone plants such as: camellias, euonymus, hollies, oaks, pecan, and fruit trees. Remember that this organic pesticide kills good bugs as well as pests.
- HOUSEPLANTS: mealybugs, spider mites, scale—spray with plant oil products or lemon joy soap at one teaspoon per gallon of water. Apply horticultural cornmeal to the soil.

Odd Jobs:
- Cover tender plants with floating row cover during extreme cold.
- Have soil tests run at that give information on organic matter, what nutrients are available to plants and the level of biological activity.
- Turn compost pile monthly or more often and keep moist. There is no reason to try to keep it warm with coverings or sunlight. The compost action is down in the center of the pile, not on the outside edge.
- Plan spring landscape improvement projects and begin hard construction activities.
- Prepare garden soil by adding compost, lava sand, and mulching bare soil. Take mowers, tillers, trimmers into shop for repairs before spring.
- Don't forget to feed the birds!

*Planting recommendations based on North Texas climate, which is zone 8. Check with your local nurseries and extension service for specific varieties and timing.

FEBRUARY

Plant*:

- Trees, shrubs, ground covers, vines, and perennials. One of the best planting months.
- Asparagus, broccoli, Brussels sprouts, cabbage, carrots, cauliflower, celery, English peas, onions, potatoes, Swiss chard and other cold-tolerant vegetables, and strawberries for harvest next spring.
- Alyssum, calendulas, cannas, daylilies, English daisies, gladiolas, Iceland poppies, larkspur, pansies, petunias, pinks, primroses, snapdragons, and other cool season annuals.
- Fruit trees, grapes, pecans and berries.
- Transplant existing landscape plants before the new spring growth begins. Do not trim to thin the plants. The idea that it compensates for root loss is nonsense.
- Divide and transplant crowded summer and fall-blooming perennials such as daisies, coneflowers, hardy hibiscus, asters, mums and salvias.

Fertilize:
First Major Fertilization of the Year

- All planting areas and turf with a natural-organic fertilizer at approximately twenty pounds per thousand square feet. If the soil is already healthy, the rate can be reduced to ten pounds per thousand square feet. For preemergent weed control, apply corn gluten meal at twenty pounds per thousand square feet.
- New organic gardeners can apply dry molasses at twenty pounds per thousand square feet.
- Cool-season flowers with earthworm castings, fish meal, cottonseed meal, alfalfa, bat guano, or other organic fertilizer at ten to twenty pounds per thousand square feet.
- Spray growing plants with Garrett Juice. Drench root zone of newly planted or transplanted plants.
- Treat problem areas with compost and compost tea.
- Feed interior plants with coffee grounds.

Prune:

- Shade and ornamental trees lightly (if necessary) to remove dead, diseased, and crossing limbs. Remove limbs that are in the way and those allowing for more light to ground plants. Do not thin out trees for no reason. Do not prune lower limbs of trees, especially newly planted ones. The low limbs and foliage are important for the development of trunk diameter
- Peaches and plums by 40-50 percent to encourage 45° angle growth. Grapes, by 80-90 percent. Other fruit trees as needed. Pecans need little to no pruning. Do not prune crape myrtle other than to remove ground sprouts.
- Evergreens and summer-flowering plants if necessary. Remove the longest canes on large shrubs to reduce height and maintain a natural appearance.

Prune (continued):

- Bush-form roses. Climbers and roses that bloom only once should be pruned after their primary flowering has ended.
- Winter-damaged foliage from liriope, purple winter creeper, Asian jasmine, and other ground covers, except for English and Persian ivy. Asian jasmine can be mowed to maintain low neat appearance.
- Remove ground covers from bases of trees to expose the soil and root flares. Remove soil from root flares if needed. Homeowners can do the work with stiff brooms or brushes.
- Remove invasive plants such as privet, non-native honeysuckle, briars and poison ivy.

Water:

- Winter annuals and any other dry soil areas as needed. Turf areas should be watered every few weeks during drought weather. Potted plants will need the most attention.

Pest Control:

- INSECTS: Giant bark aphids need no treatment needed in most cases.
- Horticultural oil can be sprayed for serious infestations of scale insects. Be sure to keep mixture shaken while using and follow label instructions carefully. Use sparingly if at all. Oil kills beneficials as well as pests.
- If needed, apply beneficial nematodes to help control grub worms, fleas, fire ants, and other pests. Remember that most grubs found in the garden are beneficial because they feed on dead organic matter rather than plant roots.
- Start the *Fruit and Pecan Tree Program* at the "pink bud" stage. See the home page of the website www.DirtDoctor.com for a print out of the most current program.
- DISEAES: Spray 3 percent hydrogen peroxide or Plant Wash.

Odd Jobs:

- Adjust and repair sprinkler system. Work on drainage problems.
- Sharpen hoes, pruning tools, and mower blades.
- Add compost and top-dressing mulch to all bare soil areas. Also add to any unhealthy looking plants.
- Turn the compost pile regularly. Add moisture during dry weather.
- Do not scalp the lawn.
- Feed and water the birds!

Planting recommendations based on North Texas climate, which is zone 8. Check with your local nurseries and extension service for specific varieties and timing.

MARCH

Plant*:

- Trees, shrubs and other permanent plants.
- Begin warm season crops such as black-eyed peas, okra, peppers, squash, tomatoes, etc. Plant a mixture of varieties and include some open-pollinated choices after last killing freeze date.
- Summer herbs: basil, lavender, lemongrass, lemon verbena, mint, oregano, sage, salad burnet, thyme, etc.
- Continue to plant cool-season annuals such as petunias and snapdragons. Begin planting warm-season types.
- Transplant as needed

Fertilize:

- All planting areas with a natural organic fertilizer at approximately twenty pounds per thousand square feet (if not done in February).
- Spray all growing plants with Garrett Juice or aerated compost tea.
- Drench the roots of newly planted plants with Garrett Juice. It makes an excellent root stimulator.

Prune:

- Finish major pruning if necessary. No flush cuts or pruning paint.
- Spring-flowering shrubs and vines only after they finish blooming: azaleas, camellias, Carolina jessamine, flowering quince, forsythia, Lady Banksia rose, spirea, weigela, wisteria, etc.
- Fruit trees just before bud break.
- Remove suckers from bases of deciduous shrubs and other plants.

Water:

- Annuals and all dry soil areas as needed.
- Potted plants as necessary.
- Turf during drought conditions.
- Add one tablespoon of apple cider vinegar to a gallon of irrigation water or one ounce of Garrett Juice.

Pest Control:

- INSECTS: Loopers and caterpillars: Spray *Bacillus thuringiensis* (Bt) biological worm spray. Add one ounce of liquid molasses per gallon of spray. Release trichogramma wasps. Apply beneficial nematodes to the soil for control of thrips on roses.
- Pillbugs, snails, slugs: Spray garlic-pepper tea and dust around plants with a mix of hot pepper, natural diatomaceous earth and cedar flakes. Spray plant oil products for serious infestations.
- Aphids: use a blast of water and a release of ladybugs. Add two ounces molasses per gallon for better results.

Pest Control (continued):

- DISEASES: Black spot, powdery mildew, and bacterial leaf spot: Spray Garrett Juice plus a cup of skim milk per gallon of spray or spray cornmeal juice. Hydrogen peroxide is even better for bacterial diseases. Plant Wash is also effective.
- Sycamore bacterial leaf scorch: Cornmeal juice or hydrogen peroxide as leaves emerge and apply the entire Sick Tree Treatment.
- Fruit trees: Spray Garrett Juice plus garlic tea at pink bud and again after flowers have fallen from the trees. Spray Garrett Juice only every two weeks. Spray Plant Wash at first sign of disease. See the *Organic Fruit and Pecan Tree Program* for more details on my website at *DirtDoctor.com*.

Odd Jobs

- Turn the compost pile and keep it moist.
- Use completed compost for bed preparation—use partially completed compost or shredded native as top-dressing mulch.
- Mulch all bare soil but do not pile mulch on the stems and trunks of plants.
- Feed and water the birds!

*Planting recommendations based on North Texas climate, which is zone 8. Check with your local nurseries and extension service for specific varieties and timing.

APRIL

Plant*:

- Trees, shrubs, ground covers, vines, and perennials.
- Warm season turf grass from plugs, solid sod, sprigs, or seed.
- Roses and other perennials.
- Fruit and pecan trees.
- Warm-season flowers including: (for sun) ageratum, columbine, copper leaf, cosmos, daisies, esperanza, firecracker fern, four nerve daisy, hummingbird bush, iris, nasturtium, penstemon, periwinkles, cosmos, portulaca, begonias, marigolds, zinnias, lantana; (for shade) caladiums, coleus, impatiens, begonias, nicotiana, hibiscus, pentas, firebush, and purple fountain grass.
- Summer herbs continue to plant in beds, pots, and hanging baskets.
- Warm-season vegetables, including melons, okra, southern peas, corn, squash, sweet potatoes, beans, cucumbers, eggplant, and tomatoes.

Fertilize:

- Summer-flowering shrubs and roses if not already done.
- Spray all plant foliage with aerated compost tea or Garrett Juice. Add garlic tea if minor insect or disease problems exist. Add fish emulsion for more power.
- Apply Garrett Juice to the soil as a root stimulator monthly to newly planted trees and shrubs.
- Treat chlorotic plants with Texas greensand or the entire Sick Tree Treatment.
- New plantings with mycorrhizal fungi products.

Prune:

- Spring-blooming vines and shrubs such as azaleas, spire, flowering quince, and forsythia immediately after bloom.
- Mums, fall asters, Mexican bush sage, and other fall blooming perennials.
- Pick-prune hedges (or light shearing if you must) to be wider at the bottom of the plant for better light and thicker growth.
- Spent blooms from roses unless you are growing them for the hips.
- Thin peach fruit to five inches apart, plums to four inches apart, apples and pears to one per cluster.

Water:

- All planting areas deeply, but infrequently, during dry periods.
- Potted plants as needed. Add Garrett Juice or aerated compost tea for fertilizer value. For additional benefit, add mycorrhizal fungi products such as Nature's Creation Quick Dissolve products.

Pest Control:
- INSECTS: Release green lacewings for control of thrips in roses, gladiolas, other flowers. Apply beneficial nematodes to the soil.
- Snails, slugs, pill bugs: spray garlic-pepper tea, or dust around plants with cedar flakes, hot pepper, and natural diatomaceous earth in dry weather. Mulch plants with pine needles or lava gravel. Spray plant oil products if necessary.
- Release trichogramma wasps for pecan casebearers and other caterpillar pests.
- Ticks, fleas, and chiggers: natural diatomaceous earths when weather is dry and apply beneficial nematodes anytime. Spray plant oil products if necessary.
- Treat peaches and plums and other fruit with the *Organic Fruit and Pecan Tree Program*. The latest version is on the home page of www.DirtDoctor.com.
- Aphids: Spray a water blast followed by release of ladybugs. Add one to two ounces of molasses for better results.
- Fire ants with beneficial nematodes. Treat mounds with Spinosad or drench with a mound drench mixture of orange oil, molasses, and compost tea.
- DISEASES: Black spot on roses: Garrett Juice plus garlic tea. See *Rose Program* also molasses/orange oil drench. Plant Wash is an effective commercial product. Spray susceptible plants on a regular basis.
- Remove the plant stress that brought the pests on, in the first place or they will be back.

Odd Jobs:
- Mow weekly and leave clippings on the lawn.
- Turn compost pile.
- Continue to add new vegetative matter and manure to existing and additional compost piles.
- Mulch all bare soil.
- Feed and water the birds!

*Planting recommendations based on North Texas climate, which is zone 8. Check with your local nurseries and extension service for specific varieties and timing.

MAY

Plant*:
- All warm season lawn grasses from plugs, sod, seed, or sprigs or by hydro-mulching. Zoysia should only be planted as solid soil. Also the tall prairie grasses from seed including big and little bluestem, Indiangrass, switchgrass, sideoats gramma, eastern gamma, etc.
- Tropical color in beds or pot including bougainvillea, mandevilla, allamanda, ixora, penta, hibiscus, and others.
- All trees and shrubs from containers. Hardened off balled and burlapped plants also. Always remove the burlap, extra soil and ropes from the top of the root balls.
- Warm-season annual color plants: lantana, begonias, zinnia, periwinkle, cosmos, caladiums, impatiens, verbena, and others.
- Perennials, including cannas, gladiolas, summer bulbs, mums, asters, and other fall perennials.
- Ground covers, including horseherb, Asian jasmine, English ivy, Persian ivy, purple wintercreeper, liriope, and ophiopogon.
- Hot-weather vegetables including southern peas, peppers, squash, okra, melons, and other warm season crops.
- Any and all of the herbs.

Fertilize:
- All annual flowers and potted plants with organic fertilizers such as Yum Yum mix. Spray Garrett Juice or aerated compost tea on all foliage every two weeks, or as time and budget allows. Drench root zones of plants for root stimulation with Garrett Juice. Add liquid fish for more fertilizer value.

Prune:
- Climbing roses, after their bloom.
- Spring-flowering shrubs, vines, and trees after they have bloomed.
- "Pinch" away the growing tips of mums weekly.
- Dead and misshapen growth.

Water:
- All planting areas deeply, but infrequently, during dry periods.
- Potted plants regularly. Add Garrett Juice or aerated compost tea.
- Add lava sand and composted mulch to help conserve water.

Pest Control

- INSECTS: Continue to release trichogramma wasps for pecan case bearer and troublesome caterpillars.
- Release green lacewings and ladybugs for general control.
- For fleas and ticks: Apply natural diatomaceous earth in-dry weather and beneficial nematodes anytime. For chiggers apply elemental sulfur at four pounds per thousand square feet or less or spray with mound drench products or other plant oil products.
- Cabbage loopers and other caterpillars: Release trichogramma wasps and as a last resort spray *Bacillus thuringiensis* (Bt) or the fire ant control formula. Add one ounce of molasses per gallon of Bt spray.
- Aphids on tender, new growth: strong water blast and release ladybugs.
- Lacebugs on azaleas, sycamores: Spray garlic-pepper tea or horticultural oil or one the mound drench products.
- Mosquitoes: Mist or spray plant oil products and apply dry or granulated garlic to site and potted plants. Treat skin and/or clothes with diluted vanilla.
- DISEASES: Brown patch or other fungal diseases: Apply horticultural or whole ground cornmeal at ten to twenty pounds per thousand square feet. Spray and/or drench soil with garlic tea. Spray Plant Wash.
- Bacterial and viral diseases: Spray 3 percent hydrogen peroxide.
- WEEDS: Hand remove or use mechanical devices. Spot spray with vinegar based products. Add one ounce of orange oil and one teaspoon of soap and one tablespoon molasses per gallon of vinegar.

Odd Jobs:

- Mow weekly and leave clippings on the lawn. *Never* catch the clippings. They don't belong in the compost pile unless there is a super abundance of them.
- Turn compost pile and continue to add new ingredients.
- Mulch all bare soil with shredded trimmings from your own property or shredded cedar. Living mulch has become my favorite. It contains shredded native tree trimmings and compost.
- Don't forget to feed and water the birds!

*Planting recommendations based on North Texas climate, which is zone 8. Check with your local nurseries and extension service for specific varieties and timing.

JUNE

Plant*:
- All warm-season grasses: Bermuda, zoysia, St. Augustine, and buffalo grasses by solid sod; Bermuda and buffalo grasses and other native grasses by seed.
- Summer annual color: amaranthus, pride of Barbados, begonias, caladiums, coleus, copperleaf, cosmos, esparangza, gomphrena, lantana, marigold, periwinkle, purslane, portulaca, verbena, zinnia, allamandas, bougainvillea, fire bush, firecracker fern, hibiscus, ixora, mandevillas, pentas, etc.
- Summer perennials: cleome, blue daze, (*Evolvulus*), cockscomb, cosmos, hardy hibiscus, and fan flower (*Scaevola*) Salvias, yellow bells, and others.
- Warm season food crops: amaranth, okra, southern peas, sweet potatoes, malbar spinach, pumpkins, and squash.
- Shrubs and trees, especially summer flowering varieties like crape myrtles.
- Fall tomatoes and other fall vegetable crops.

Fertilize:
- Avoid all synthetic fertilizers, especially nitrogen only products like 24-0-0.

Second Major Fertilization of the Year
- All planting areas with organic fertilizer. This should be the second major fertilization of the year. Use about twenty pounds of fertilizer per thousand square feet. To give plants an extra boosts, use fish meal or corn gluten meal. Add mycorrhizal products such as Nature's Creation.
- Spray all plantings and lawns with Garrett Juice every two weeks or at least once a month.
- Iron and general trace mineral deficiency results in yellowed leaves with dark green veins on the youngest growth. Drench soil with Garrett Juice, Texas greensand. Magnesium products will also help. Use high-calcium lime for calcium deficiency.
- Apply the Sick Tree Treatment to any ailing trees and other woody plants.

Prune:
- Long erratic shoots from abelia, elaeagnus, lady banks roses, etc.
- Remove spent blooms and shear flowering plants by one-third that has started to decline. Don't wait until they have completely stopped blooming.
- Blackberries to remove fruiting canes after harvest. Prune new canes to three feet in height to encourage side branching.
- Dead and damaged wood from trees, shrubs, as needed.

Water:
- All planting areas deeply, but infrequently, during dry periods.
- Potted plants regularly. Daily watering needed for some plants. Add an ounce per gallon of Garrett Juice at least once a month.

Pest Control:

- Yellow lower leaves on tomatoes—spray garlic and/or cornmeal juice. Plant Wash may be even better.
- Spider mites: Spray Garrett Juice or any seaweed product as needed.
- Fleas, ticks, chiggers: dust with natural diatomaceous earth in dry weather and release beneficial nematodes anytime.
- Gray leaf spot—reduce fertilizers and spray garlic and/or corn meal juice with Garrett Juice.
- Bagworms and other caterpillars: Release trichogramma wasps and spray if needed with *Bacillus thuringiensis* (Bt). Spinosad and mound drench products containing orange oil can also be used. Garrett Juice plus two ounces of orange oil per gallon of spray is also effective.
- Scale insects, including mealybugs: Spray plant oil products or mound drench products.
- Black spot on roses, mildew, and other fungi: Spray Garrett Juice plus garlic tea or diluted skim milk and drench the soil with garlic tea or apply dry granulated garlic See Home Page for the entire Organic Rose Program. Spray Plant Wash.
- Weeds: Hand remove and work on improving soil health. Spot spray vinegar-based products.
- Lacebugs, elm leaf beetles green June bugs, etc. Spray garlic pepper tea, summer-weight horticultural oil, plant oil products, or mound drench products containing orange oil. Spinosad products will also work on this and other insect pests.

Odd Jobs:

- Mow weekly and leave clippings on the lawn.
- Turn compost pile as needed.
- Mulch all bare soil, do not pile mulch on trunks and stems of plants.
- Feed and water the birds!

*Planting recommendations based on North Texas climate, which is zone 8. Check with your local nurseries and extension service for specific varieties and timing.

JULY

Plant*:

- Prepare new beds with quality compost, expanded shale, lava sand, greensand, dry molasses, and horticultural or whole ground corn meal. Work amendments into the native soil. If possible, prepare beds under trees with the air spade to prevent injury to roots.
- Color for fall including: asters, celosia, cosmos, marigolds, morning glory, Joseph's coat, ornamental grasses, Mexican bush sage, and zinnias.
- Container-grown nursery stock and field-grown trees.
- Warm-seasonal lawn grasses.
- Herbs such as basil, oregano, thyme, lemon grass, lemon verbena, etc.
- Tomatoes, peppers, melons, and other warm-season vegetables for fall garden. Plant pumpkin seeds around July 4 for Jack-o' Lanterns for Halloween. Also plant beans, black-eyed peas, cantaloupe, chard, cucumber, egg plant, New Zealand and Malabar spinach, and summer and winter squash.
- Wildflower seed—better now than to wait until fall.

Fertilize

- Avoid synthetic, high nitrogen, salt fertilizers especially nitrogen-only choices.
- All planting areas with organic fertilizers, if not done in June
- Use greensand for iron deficiency and other trace mineral deficiencies.
- Use high calcium lime for low pH soils and calcium deficiencies. Also drench with fireplace ashes and water. Use one rounded tablespoon per gallon of water.
- Foliar feed with Garrett Juice or aerated composted tea on all foliage. Drench the soil around plants as well.
- Roses, to encourage fall blooms.

Prune:

- Dead or damaged limbs.
- Flowering plants to remove spent flower heads and encourage new flower production.
- Trees and shrubs if needed—no flush cuts.
- Lightly prune roses.
- Prune flower heads off crape myrtles.

Water:

- Water carefully and efficiently during drought periods.
- All planting areas deeply but infrequently during dry periods.
- Outdoor container plants daily, others as needed.

Pest Control

- INSECTS: Cinch bugs: Dust natural diatomaceous earth or spray the orange oil-based fire ant control mound drench formula.
- Elms leaf beetles, lace bugs: Spray summer-weight horticultural oil or orange oil based mound drench products. Use *Bacillus thuringiensis* (Bt) on infested plants only.
- Spider mites: Spray garlic pepper tea or any spray that contains liquid seaweed.
- Fire ants: Drench with one of the mound drench products. Apply Spinosad product. Apply beneficial nematodes.
- Fleas, ticks, chiggers, Bermuda mites: Dust natural diatomaceous earth during dry weather. Spray orange oil mound drench products and apply beneficial nematodes anytime, but especially during wet weather. Dust with very light amounts of sulfur in alkaline soils.
- Webworms, bagworms, leaf rollers, and other worms of moths and butterflies: spray *Bacillus thuringiensis* (Bt) with one ounce of orange oil per gallon. Add one ounce of liquid molasses per gallon of spray and spray at dusk. Release trichogramma wasps next year when leaves first emerge in the spring.
- Scale insects on euonymus, hollies, and camellias: Spray horticultural oil or fire ant mound drench formula or remove the unadapted plants. Southern gardeners should avoid evergreen euonymus.
- Mosquitoes—Spray garlic tea and apply dry granulated garlic to the soil and pots.
- DISEASES: Spray hydrogen peroxide or Plant Wash.
- WEEDS: Hand remove or use mechanical devices. Spray vinegar based herbicides if needed.

Odd Jobs:

- Mow weekly or as needed and leave clippings on the lawn.
- Turn compost pile, add new ingredients, and start new piles. Add molasses to piles to stimulate biological activity and eliminate problems with fire ants.
- Mulch all bare soil with composted or other shredded native tree trimmings or other coarse textured natural material. Avoid pine bark, cypress, dyed woods, rubber and plastic materials.
- Feed and water the birds!

*Planting recommendations based on North Texas climate, which is zone 8. Check with your local nurseries and extension service for specific varieties and timing.

AUGUST

Plant*:
- Plant portulaca, purslane, marigold, zinnia, copper canyon daisy, wild-flowers, and ornamental grasses for immediate color. Many great types of salvia are available. User spider lilies, fall crocus, fall amaryllis, mums, and asters for later flowers.
- Fall vegetable garden plants, especially the warm weather veggies.
- Planting warm-season lawn grasses as needed—buffalo, Bermuda, St. Augustine, zoysia.
- Horseherb, liriope, ophiopogon, Persian Ivy, and other ground covers in shady areas where turf is struggling.
- Wildflowers seed if you haven't already.

Prune:
- Declining flowering plants to encourage more blooms.
- Dead and damaged wood from shrubs and trees. No flush cuts or pruning dressings or paints.

Fertilize:
- Foliar feed all planting with Garrett Juice, compost tea or mycorrhizal products such as Nature's Creation. Also drench the soil of any new or struggling plants.
- If your soil is not yet healthy, apply dry molasses at a rate of ten pounds per thousand square feet. Do not fertilize wildflower areas.

Water:
- Water deeply and as infrequently as possible. Your garden and landscape will usually need more water this month than any other.
- Potted plants and hanging baskets need water daily. Expanded shale and/or lava sand added to the soil as mulch will greatly help hold moisture and reduce watering needs.
- Be especially careful of azalea beds and other sensitive plants.

Pest Control:

- INSECTS: Grubworms: Good soil culture is the best control. Apply molasses and beneficial nematodes and needed.
- Chinch bugs: Dust natural diatomaceous earth or spray one of the orange oil-based pest control products or another of the plant oil products. Do not use pyrethrum products for this or any other pest.
- Aphids: Garrett Juice and garlic tea. Water blast and release of lady bugs. Add molasses to water spray at two ounces per gallon of spray. Apply Sick Tree Treatment.
- Fire ants: Dust natural diatomaceous earth or spray one of the orange oil-based pest control products or any other of the plant oil products. Apply beneficial nematodes. Broadcast orange or grapefruit peelings and pulp. Horticultural cornmeal also helps. The application of grits continues to provide strong reports. Spinosad products are also effective.
- Chewing insects: Dust natural diatomaceous earth or spray Garret Juice plus garlic pepper tea. Spray plant oil products such as Bioganic or Eco-EXEMPT if needed. Add 2 ounces per gallon of orange oil or d-limonene for the hard to control insects.
- Cabbage loopers and other caterpillars: Release trichogramma wasps and spray *Bacillus thuringiensis* (Bt) at dusk with molasses added at one to two ounces per gallon of spray.
- Mosquitoes: Spray or mist one of the plant oil products (not pyrethrum) and apply dry, minced garlic at ten to twenty pounds per thousand square feet.
- Borers in peaches, plums, and other fruit trees: Use the Organic Fruit and Pecan Tree Program (download from www.DirtDoctor.com).
- Borers: Apply d-limonene or orange oil to the affected parts of the trunks. Mix into of a 50/50 solution with water. Seal the holes with Tree Goop.
- DISEASES: Spray hydrogen peroxide or Plant Wash.

Odd Jobs

- Mow weekly and leave clippings on the lawn.
- Turn compost pile.
- Spray weeds in walks, driveways, and terraces with vinegar. Use 10 percent or 100 grain with one ounce of orange oil, one tablespoon molasses and one teaspoon of liquid soap per gallon. Carefully spot spray in beds and turf.
- Don't forget to feed and water the birds!

*Planting recommendations based on North Texas climate, which is zone 8. Check with your local nurseries and extension service for specific varieties and timing.

SEPTEMBER

Plant*:

- Wildflower seeds if you didn't plant them at the best time in summer.
- Finish warm-season lawn grass plantings of Bermuda and zoysia by seed no later than early September. Solid sod can be planted any time. Cool season grasses such as ryegrass, fescue, and blue grass can be planted in the later part of the month.
- Transplant established spring-flowering bulbs, iris, daylilies, daisies, and peonies.
- Fall blooming perennials such as asters and mums. Hardy perennials, especially spring blooming plants. Divide spring blooming perennials if necessary
- Cool-season vegetables, including broccoli, cauliflower, Brussels sprouts, cabbage, beets, turnips, spinach, potatoes, lettuce, carrots, beets, radishes, and English peas.

Fertilize:
Third Major Fertilization of the Year

- All planting areas with an organic fertilizer at approximately ten to twenty pounds per thousand square feet. Corn gluten meal can be used to help control annual winter weeds such as bluegrass, dandelion, henbit, fescue grass, ryegrass, and *Poa annua*.
- Foliar feed all plants and lawns with Garrett Juice or compost tea. Also drench the soil for new and problems plants.
- Avoid all synthetic fertilizers but especially "weed and feed" types and the "nitrogen only" types. Remember that the only complete balanced fertilizers are organic. Others contain no carbon and poor compliments of trace minerals.

Prune

- Root-prune wisterias that failed to bloom in the past.
- Shade and ornamental trees if needed. Make no flush cuts and use no pruning paint.
- Remove spent blooms of summer flowering perennials if you haven't already.
- Remove surface tree roots if you must but no more than 20 percent of root system per year. It's best to leave the roots and add shredded tree trimming mulch or convert from grass to groundcovers.

Water

- Water deeply, but only as needed during dry spells.
- Potted plants and hanging baskets regularly. Add Garrett Juice as a root stimulator for better performance.

Pest Control:

- Brown patch or take all patch in St. Augustine: Apply horticultural cornmeal at ten to twenty pounds per thousand square feet. For follow-up applications, use dry or liquid garlic, potassium bicarbonate. or cornmeal juice. Dry granulated garlic at two pounds per thousand square feet. Also works well.
- Webworms, tent caterpillars: *Bacillus thuringiensis* (Bt) as a last resort on infected plants only. Spinosad is also effective. Make a note to release trichogramma wasps next spring.
- Grubworms—apply beneficial nematodes if necessary, but realize that only 10 percent of the grubs you see are harmful to plants. Dry molasses will also help.
- Cabbage loopers on broccoli, Brussels sprouts, cauliflower, cabbage: Spray *Bacillus thuringiensis* (Bt). Release trichogramma wasps prior to this time next year.
- Aphids on tender, new fall growth—spray garlic tea or water blast followed by release of ladybugs. Add one to two ounces of molasses per gallon of spray. Spinosad can also be used.
- Fire ants—Drench mounds with orange oil based mound drench or plant oil products and apply beneficial nematodes. Apply spinosad products for problem infestations.
- DISEASES: Black spot and powdery mildew: Spray garlic-pepper tea and see the Organic Rose Program on the website, www.DirtDoctor.com.
- Chlorosis (yellow leaves, dark green veins, newest growth first): Apply the entire Sick Tree Treatment and add Epsom salts or sul-po-mag if magnesium is deficient in the soil. Greensand can help because it contains many trace minerals. Iron may not be the only one deficient. The key is to stimulate the biological activity of the soil so that the "tied-up" minerals in the soil are made available to plants.
- WEEDS: Chemicals pushers recommend MSMA. It's an idiotic recommendation. The product contains an arsenic compound. They also recommend the dangerous 2, 4–D products for broadleaf weeds. They also recommend products like Manage for other weeds. These chemicals will severely injure or kill trees. Image is a waste of money and can do damage. Organic weed control results from healthy soil, thick healthy plants, fertilizing with corn gluten meal and spot spraying natural organic weed controls.

Odd Jobs

- Mow weekly and leave clippings on the lawn.
- Turn the compost pile.
- Feed and water the birds!

*Planting recommendations based on North Texas climate, which is zone 8. Check with your local nurseries and extension service for specific varieties and timing.

OCTOBER

Plant*:

- Cool-season, leaf and root crops such as beets, Brussels sprouts, cabbage, carrots, collards, garlic, lettuce, spinach, strawberries, and turnips.
- Dianthus, English daisies, flowering cabbage garlic, Iceland poppies, kale, nasturtium, pansies, pinks, snapdragons, violas, and wallflowers.
- All the perennial herbs as well as coriander, dill, and parsley.
- Transplant established spring-flowering bulbs, iris, daylilies, daisies, peonies, etc. if necessary.
- Hardy perennials, especially spring flowering plants.
- Finish warm-season lawn grass plantings by seed by early October. Quality solid sod can be planted anytime that quality grass is available. Be sure to wet the soil of the sod before planting. Apply a thin layer of compost to the surface after planting.
- Wildflower seeds if you haven't planted them already.
- Trees, shrubs, vines, and spring-and summer-flowering perennials.
- Cool-season grasses such as rye and fescue. It is also time to plant clover, vetch, Austin winter peas and other cool season crops.

Fertilize:

- Broadcast dry molasses for any plants not looking well. Feed all planting areas with an organic fertilizer at approximately ten to twenty pounds per thousand square feet.
- Foliar-feed all planting areas and lawns with compost tea or Garrett Juice. Make sure to include seaweed in whatever mix you use. Drench potted plants with the same mixture. Liquid fish should be added for more punch.
- Feed trees by treating the soil surface or top few inches. Avoid "deep root" feeding. "Root zone" feeding is a better term.

Prune:

- Tree limbs that are broken, diseased or in the way. Dangerous limbs that might fall. Do not make flush cuts and use no pruning paint or wound dressing. Do not over-prune any trees.
- Root-prune wisterias that have failed to bloom. This may or may not help.
- Remove spent blooms of summer flowering perennials.
- Do not prune knees from bald cypress trees—they are part of the root system. Instead change the root zone areas from grass to ground cover or mulch.

Pest Control:

- INSECTS: Spray aerated compost tea.
- DISEASES: Spray Plant Wash or hydrogen peroxide.
- WEEDS: Spray weeds and grass around tree trunks with vinegar. Use 9–10 percent with one ounce orange oil, one tablespoon molasses, and one teaspoon liquid soap per gallon. Fatty acid products can also be helpful.

Water:

- All plants deeply during dry spells. Greensand at forty pounds per thousand square feet. Greensand is important because it contains many trace minerals. Iron may not be (probably isn't) the only deficiency.

Odd Jobs:

- Mulch all bare soil with shredded tree trimmings. Shredded material from your own property is best. If it is partially composted or mixed with compost, it is better. Rubber, colored wood, cypress, and pine bark should be avoided.
- Mow weekly and leave the clippings on the lawn. Those with buffalo grass can mow less often, as little as once a year.
- Build new compost piles, turn old ones, and water dry ones.
- Use quality compost and other organic amendments to prepare new planting beds. See the Organic Guides on the home page of www.DirtDoctor.com for complete bed preparation details.
- To reflower a poinsettia, give it uninterrupted darkness fourteen hours each day and ten hours of bright light each day until December. It's better to buy new plants each year.
- Use compost or shredded tree trimmings as a top-dressing mulch for ornamentals and vegetables.
- Feed and water the birds!

*Planting recommendations based on North Texas climate, which is zone 8. Check with your local nurseries and extension service for specific varieties and timing.

NOVEMBER

Plant*:

- Trees, shrubs vines, ground covers and tough perennials.
- Spring bulbs, including daffodils and grape hyacinths. Pre-cool tulips and Dutch hyacinths for forty-five days at about 40° prior to planting in December.
- Spring and summer flowering perennials, including daisies, daylilies, iris, lilies, lythrum, thrift, etc.
- Finish planting cool season spring-flowering annuals including alyssum, California and Iceland poppies, dianthus and English daisies, flowering cabbage and kale, Johnny jump ups, pansies, petunias, pinks, snapdragons.
- Finish planting cool-season grasses such as rye and fescue, also clover and vetch.
- Dwarf white clover in bare areas as needed.
- Finish planting cool season vegetable crops and herbs.

Fertilize:

- Apply one-half inch of compost to poorly performing turf areas.
- Bulbs, annuals, and perennials with earthworm castings, other quality composts, and other gentle, organic fertilizers.
- Indoor plants with earthworm castings, lava sand, and other low-odor, organic fertilizers.
- Foliar feed actively growing plants with aerated compost, fish, and seaweed or Garret Juice Plus.
- Cool season grasses and other growing plants with organic fertilizer at one-half rates.

Prune:

- Remove all vines from trees, limbs, trunks, and root flares.
- Remove ground covers, grasses, and soils from the bases of trees.
- Begin major tree pruning if needed. Protect the branch collars by never making flush cuts. Remove dead limbs if possible before leaves fall. Do not over prune.
- Pick-prune shrubs to remove longest shoots, if needed. Lightly sheer unruly plants.
- Remove spent blooms on annuals and perennials or leave the seed heads on flowering plants for the birds.
- Cut off tops of brown perennials. Remove spent annuals but leave roots in the soil.

Water:

- All planting areas at least once if no rain. Add one tablespoon (one ounce) of apple cider vinegar to each gallon of water used on indoor and outdoor potted plants—or at least as often as possible.

Pests:

- INSECTS: Check the roots of removed annuals and other suspicious plants for nematodes (knots on the roots). Treat infected soil with biostimulants, molasses, compost, and/or citrus pulp.
- Check house plants for spider mites, scale, and aphids. Apply horticultural cornmeal or dry granulated garlic to the soil. Spray as needed with bio-stimulants and mild soap products such as Plant Wash and seaweed products. Use plant oils and light weight horticultural oils as a last resort.
- Watch lawn for signs of grubworm damage. Grass will be loose and not con-nected to the soil. Treat with dry molasses or beneficial nematodes. These insects are rarely a problem for organic gardeners with healthy soil.
- DISEASES: If brown patch disease is still showing in turf, treat with horticul-tural or whole ground cornmeal and drench with garlic tea if the problem persists. Applying dry granulated garlic has also proven to be effective. Spray-ing Plant Wash is also effective.
- WEEDS: Hand remove.

Odd Jobs:

- Pick tomatoes the day before the first freeze. Let them ripen indoors.
- Put spent annuals and other vegetative matter into the compost piles. Mulch fallen leaves into the turf. Put excesses in beds or in the compost pile.
- Add native tree trimmings mulch to cover all bare soil. Do not till or plow once healthy soil has been developed in the vegetable garden.
- Mulch all bare ornamental beds for winter protection.
- Turn compost piles as time allows.
- Feed and water the birds!

* Planting recommendations based on North Texas climate. Check with your local garden centers and extension services for specific varieties and timing in your area.

DECEMBER

Plant*:

- Cool season annuals and hardy perennials. Delphiniums, larkspur, and poppies from seed. Many cool season transplant choices are available.
- Trees, shrubs, vines, ground covers, and other crops such as arugula, cabbage, kale, chard, greens, spinach, and lettuce. Carrots and garlic can still be planted.
- Herb transplants including lavender, oregano, rosemary, rue, sage, parsley, coriander, dill, and fennel. Dill and fennel may need some freeze protection
- Living Christmas trees (after use) that are adapted to the area's climate and soils.
- Spring bulbs, including tulips and hyacinths.
- Transplant shrubs and trees.

Fertilize:

- Avoid all synthetic fertilizers, of course.
- Cool season annuals in beds and pots. Use Garrett Juice as a soil drench fertilizer.
- Greenhouse plants if needed with organic fertilizers, earthworm castings and lava sand.
- Houseplants, once during winter, with earthworm castings, lava sand, and other odorless organic fertilizers. Coffee grounds are one good choice. Add apple cider vinegar at one tablespoon to one ounce per gallon at each watering. Nature's Creation Quick Dissolve Indoor Plant Tablets is a product that is convenient and effective.
- Winter grasses with mild organic fertilizer at one-half the rate, usually ten pounds per thousand square feet.
- See the Organic Fruit and Pecan Tree Program on the home page www.DirtDoctor.com for details on these trees.

Prune:

- Do not prune the tops of crape myrtles. The seed pods are decorative and some birds like the seed.
- Evergreens, to adjust the appearance.
- Do not make flush cuts and do not apply pruning paint to any plants.
- Shade trees to remove dead, damaged, and out of place limbs. Do not prune just to "thin out" trees. Trimming can be done to avoid crowding and to allow more light to under story plants.
- Cut off tops of spent perennials if not already done. Leave roots in the ground.
- Wait till the end of the winter to prune fruit trees and grapes. Best timing for them is just before bud break to prevent premature flowering.
- Use the dormant months to remove ground covers from the bases of plants and vines completely from all trees. If soil is on the root flares and trunks of trees, remove the soil very carefully with slow water, a stiff broom, and a shop vac. It's best to hire an arborist to do the work with the air spade.

Water:

- Potted plants as needed.
- Any dry areas to help protect against desiccation and winter cold injury.
- Add apple cider vinegar at one tablespoon to one ounce per gallon, time permitting

Pests:

- INSECTS: Spray houseplants with liquid seaweed, mild soap, and bio-stimulants to control scale, mealy bugs, spider mites, and other insects. Mild orange oil-based mound drench solutions can also be used.
- Bark aphids on trees look scary but normally need no treatment.
- Spray heavy infestations scale insects on shade and fruit trees with horticultural oil. Not recommended except in extreme cases. Sprays will kill beneficial insects and microbes.
- Avoid all toxic chemical pesticides, as usual.
- DISEASES: Spray garlic tea on plants with fungal diseases. Apply dry granulated garlic to the soil for addition control. Spray Plant Wash.
- WEEDS: Remember that henbit, clover, and other wildflowers are beautiful, so don't worry about spraying them in most cases. If you must, spray vinegar, orange oil, and soap between Christmas and New Years. See appendix for formula.
- Cut mistletoe out of trees. Remove infested limbs if possible. Apply the Sick Tree Treatment. Also apply the Sick Tree Treatment to other stressed trees such as those with heavy infestations of galls.

Odd Jobs:

- Continue to mulch leaves into the turf.
- Cover tender plants before freezes with floating row cover. Potted plants can be covered with large trash cans.
- Pick tomatoes the night before first freeze, unless they are already gone.
- Clean and oil tools before storing for winter.
- Run mower, trimmer engines dry of gasoline. Drain and change oil. Take to repair shop now to avoid the spring rush.
- Mulch all bare soil. Apply a thin layer of compost followed by shredded native tree trimmings.
- Turn compost piles as time allows. Add molasses to speed up break down.
- Apply lava or decomposed granite on icy paving. Do not use chemical de-icers, salt or synthetic fertilizers.
- Feed and water the birds!

Planting recommendations based on North Texas climate, which is zone 8. Check with your local nurseries and extension service for specific varieties and timing.

NATURAL ORGANIC PEST CONTROL

The answer to pest problems is not in a bag of poisonous chemicals, but in a better understanding of the laws of Nature and a desire to work with these laws.

—Malcolm Beck, San Antonio 1988

Ever wondered how insects were kept under control or why plants weren't devoured by destructive insects before man started to "chemically control" the environment? The answer lies in the fact that nature has a balanced, natural order.

With the proliferation of chemicals during the twentieth century, many beneficial insects have been killed along with the harmful insects. Generally, the harmful ones will reestablish themselves more quickly than will the beneficial ones, and plant loss accelerates. Encouraging the beneficial insects to be established again is a primary goal of an organic program. However, there are many safe or low-toxicity products available for transition from a toxic chemical program to a natural organic program that will reduce the harmful effects to beneficial insect populations.

A report by the scientific journal *Bioscience* says that only about 1 percent of the pesticides applied to plants ever reaches its ultimate destination—the pest insects. The other 99 percent pollute and poison the air, soil, water, good bugs, animals, and man.

This section is divided into two parts—one on harmful insects and one on beneficial insects. First, the beneficial insects and how they can help keep the harmful insects under control. After all, the pests under control is all that is really needed, since the surviving ones will serve as a lure for the beneficial insects. I'll then go over the major harmful insects, along with how to control them, primarily with biological products. I no longer recommend the common botanical products. Pesticides like pyrethrum, rotonone, sabadilla are toxic and don't last to kill insects. Their toxicity is only strong while you are handling the products. Plus, there are more effective means.

BENEFICIAL INSECTS

It would be impossible to cover all the beneficial insects because somewhere around 98 percent of the world's insects are beneficial. It could be argued that even the destructive bugs are good because they identify and help eliminate weak and ill-adapted plants.

The best way to control troublesome insects is to allow them to control themselves. Nature provides beautiful checks and balances if we allow them to function. Friendly bugs are being used more and more to help control destructive insects in vegetable gardens, stored grain, greenhouses, and orchards. Parasitic mites and wasps are being used to control houseflies, barnyard flies, and fire ants. Earthworms, centipedes, and millipedes are not technically insects, but they are basically beneficial, especially earthworms. Centipedes and millipedes are helpful because they aerate the soil, produce nutrients, and help break down organic material. If they come inside, vacuum them.

A critical element of an organic program is the establishment and maintenance of biodiversity. That means the vegetable garden and landscaping need to have a healthy and dynamic mix of insects, plants, animals, and birds. Man needs to fit into that puzzle as well. Here's some information on the insects and other critters that can help you maintain your gardens.

See the *Texas Bug Book* by Malcolm Beck and Howard Garrett for additional information on using beneficial insects and controlling insect pests.

BENEFICIAL INSECTS

Ground Beetles

One-third of all animals and 40 percent of all insects are beetles. Beetles have hard, opaque wing covers that meet in a straight line down the middle of their backs. The ground beetles are important predators of plant-eating insects. They usually feed at night on soft-bodied larvae such as cankerworms, tent caterpillars, slugs and snails. Soldier beetles feed on aphids, grasshopper eggs, cucumber beetles, and various caterpillars.

Ladybugs

larva

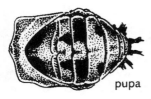

pupa

adult

Ladybird beetle is the proper term, but these little friends are best known as ladybugs. They are the most popular and most universally known beneficial insects. There are several hundred different kinds in North America and all are beneficial should be protected. The convergent ladybug—orange with black spots—is the most available commercially.

Yellow ladybug eggs are visible in the winter and early spring in clusters on the backs of leaves and on the trunks of trees. The adult ladybug can eat two hundred aphids per day, the larvae seventy to a hundred per day. The larvae and the adult beetles eat large quantities of aphids and other small, soft-bodied insects such as scale, thrips, and mealy bugs. They should be released after aphids are visible and at night after the foliage has been sprinkled with water. Let a few out at a time to see if they are hungry. It they fly away, put them in the refrigerator for a day or two and try again later after they have used up their stored food. Ladybugs will store in the refrigerator for a few days (35-45° is best for storage). They will remain dormant and alive under these cool temperatures, although storage tends to dry them out and a few will die. They will naturalize on your site if chemical sprays are eliminated.

For ladybugs to mature and lay eggs, they need a nectar and pollen source, such as flowering plants. Legumes such as peas, beans, clover, and alfalfa are especially good. To make an artificial food, dilute a little honey with a small amount of water and mix in a little brewer's yeast or bee pollen. Streak tiny amounts of this mixture on small pieces of waxed paper, and fasten these to plants. Replace these every five or six days, or when they become moldy. Keep any extra food refrigerated between feedings. The ladybug's favorite real food is the aphid.

If ladybugs are released indoors or in a greenhouse, you might want to screen off any openings to prevent their escape.

Fireflies (Lightning Bugs)

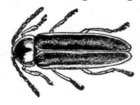

The firefly is a fascinating insect that produces a light by releasing luciferin from its abdomen to combine with oxygen. When conditions are right, the male flashes his light every six seconds to be answered by the female two seconds later. Firefly larvae feed on snails, slug, cutworms, and mites. Plus they are just wonderful to see.

Green Lacewings

eggs

Green lacewings are beautiful, fragile, light-green or brown insects with lustrous, yellow eyes. Adults are approximately one-half inch long, hold their wings up tent-like when at rest, and feed on honeydew, nectar, and pollen. The adults really aren't terribly beneficial. They just fly around, look pretty, and mate. They actually do help with pollination of plants. The larvae, on the other hand, are voracious eaters of aphids, red spider mites, thrips, mealybugs, cottony cushion scale, and many worms.

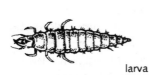

larva

Lacewing larvae (also known as "aphid lions") emerge from eggs, which appear on the end of thin white filaments attached to leaves or stems. The larvae pupates by spinning cocoons with silken thread. Adults emerge in about five days by cutting a hole in the cocoon.

cocoon

If it is inconvenient to release the lacewing immediately after purchase, the eggs or larvae may be refrigerated for a few days, but do not allow to freeze, 38° to 45°F will delay development but not hurt the eggs.

adult

Eggs and larvae can be hand sprinkled wherever harmful insects exist or are suspected. Even if you put them in the wrong place, they will search almost a hundred feet for their first meal. One of the best ways to distribute lacewing eggs and larvae is with a pill bottle with a small hole in the cap. A salt shaker will work, but you have to increase the size of the holes. A thimble will hold about ten thousand eggs. Releasing the green lacewing from a card or cup mounted in a tree will keep the fire ants from getting them before they do their work. It helps to put a sticky material such as Tanglefoot on the trunk of the tree to block the ant's access. Apply it to paper wrapped around the trunk to prevent girdling damage to the trunk.

Lacewing larvae are gray in color, look like tiny alligators and mature in two to three weeks. Biweekly releases are ideal. Flowering plants attract green lacewings; buckwheat is especially good. If you aren't spraying toxic pesticides, these helpful insects will be on your property. They will often be seen fluttering around lights on the porch.

Predatory Mites

Adult predatory mites are orange in color. The immature stages are pale salmon color. They can be differentiated from the "red" two-spotted spider mites by the lack of spots on either side. Bodies are pear-shaped, and the front legs are longer than those of pest mites. Predatory mites move about quickly when disturbed or exposed to bright light, and they multiply twice as quickly as pest mites do, with the females laying about fifty eggs. They eat from five to twenty eggs or mites per day.

Release predatory mites at the first sign of spider mite damage. For heavy infestations, you will probably need to reduce the populations of pest mites with organic sprays such as Garrett Juice plus orange oil at two ounces per gallon of spray.

Praying Mantids (Also Called Praying Mantises)

These fierce looking, and acting, critters will eat almost any insect, especially caterpillars, grass-hoppers, beetles, and other damaging pests. Be careful not to confuse the egg cases with the asp or puss caterpillar, which is a soft, hairy insect with a powerful sting. The praying mantid egg case looks very similar, but is hard like paper-mache. The only negative about praying mantids is that they also eat beneficial insects. They don't usually eat ladybugs, however, because ladybugs are bitter. Don't believe me? Try one!

Spiders

Most spiders are beneficial and harmless—with the strong exceptions of the black widow and brown recluse. Brown recluse are normally found indoors. You'll rarely see a brown recluse because they seek out dark corners in closets, etc., and move about at night. The female black widow is easy to identify by the red hourglass on her abdomen. Beware of her because her venomous sting is very powerful and can cause illness and even death. The puny little male isn't much trouble; in fact, the female devours him after mating.

Wasps

All wasps and mud daubers are beneficial. Among their favorite foods are tent caterpillars and webworms that often disfigure trees. Wasps will sting only if you threaten them or the mud dauber—only if you grab it! So don't! Trichogramma and other friendly wasps don't sting at all. The mud dauber's favorite food is the black widow spider. It's also good for controlling flies in horse stables. Brachonid wasps kill pests by laying their eggs in hosts like hornworms, codling moths, and aphids. The large cicada killer wasps look ferocious but are quite harmless unless grabbed. So once again, don't do that!

Trichogramma Wasps

Trichogramma wasps or "moth egg parasites" are used to control pecan casebearer, cutworms, moths, cabbage worms, tomato hornworms, corn earworms, and other caterpillars. They are almost microscopic parasitic wasps which attack more than two hundred types of worm pests. The trichogramma wasp stings the pest worm egg and deposits its own egg inside. The egg hatches and the larva feeds on and kills the pest.

Early application of trichogramma before a problem has been diagnosed is the ideal way to begin a pest control program. Weekly or biweekly releases throughout the early growing season are ideal. The first release should be made when trees start to leaf out in the spring.

Whitefly Parasites

Whitefly parasites can help to deter serious damage to tomatoes, cucumbers, and ornamental plants. *Encarsia formosa* is a small, efficient parasite of the whitefly. It is about the size of a spider mite. It attacks the whiteflies in the immature stages, laying eggs in the third and fourth stages, while feeding off the first and second stages. Early application of *Encarsia formosa* prior to heavy infestations is recommended. Parasites should be released at the first sign of whiteflies.

Nematodes

Beneficial nematodes are microscopic roundworms used to control cutworms, armyworms, corn rootworms, cabbage loopers, Colorado potato beetles, grubworms, termites, fleas, fire ants, and other soil pests. Nematodes enter the insect pest through the mouth or other body openings. Once inside the host, the nematodes feed and reproduce until the food supply is gone. Then hordes of nematodes emerge in search of new victims. Sounds pretty gross, doesn't it? Early applications prior to heavy pest infestations, followed by monthly follow up applications, are best. Heterorhabditis (Heteros) are best for grubworm control. Steinernema (Steiners) work for grubs but are better for moths.

Other beneficial insects include syrphid flies, parasitoids, big-eyed bugs, pirate bugs, and many, many others. For more details on beneficial insects see the *Texas Bug Book*.

> *And, of course, anyplace you use beneficial insects, you'll want to avoid spraying pesticides—even the organic pesticides that kill should have very limited use.*

SOURCES FOR BENEFICIAL BUGS

A-1 Unique Insect Control — *www.a-1unique.com* -5504 Sperry Drive, Citrus Heights, CA 95621, (916) 961-7945, Fax (916) 967-7082

American Insectaries, Inc. — *www.betterbugs.com* - 30805 Rodriguez Road, Escondido, CA 92026, (760) 751-1436

Arbico — *www.arbico-organics.co*m - P.O. Box 4247, Tucson, AZ 85738, 800-827-2847

Beneficial Insectary — *www.insectary.com* — 9664 Tanqueray Court, Redding, CA 96003, (530)-226-6300 or 800-477-3715

Biofac Crop Care- *www.biofac.com* -PO Box 87, Mathis, TX 78368, 1-800-233-4914

BioLogic — *www.biologicco.com* -Springtown Road, P.O. Box 177, Willow Hill, PA 17271, (717) 349-2789

Gulf Coast BioTech Controls — *www.gulfcoast.com* — 72 West Oaks, Huntsville, Texas 77340, (800) 524-1958.

Harmony Farm Supply — *www.harmonyfarm.com* -P.O. Box 460, Graton, CA 95444, (707) 823-9125

Hydro-Gardens, Inc. — *www.hydro-gardens.com* - P.O. Box 25845, Colorado Springs, CO 80936 (800) 634-6362

Kunafin Trichogramma Industries — *www.kunafin.com* - Route 1, Box 39, Quemado, TX 78877, (800) 832-1113, Fax (830) 757-1468

M&R Durango — *www.goodbug.com* - P.O. Box 886, Bayfield, CO 81122, (800) 526-4075

Nature's Control — *www.naturescontrol.com* — P.O. Box 35Medford, OR 97501 (541) 245-6033

Peaceful Valley Farm Supply — *www.groworganic.com* - P.O. Box 2209, Grass Valley, CA 95945, (916) 272-4769, (888)-784-1722

Planet Natural - *www.planetnatural.com* - P.O. Box 3146, Bozeman, MT 59772, (406) 587-5891, (800) 289-6656

Rincon-Vitova Insectaries, Inc. — *www.rinconvitova.com* -P.O. Box 1555, Ventura, CA 93022, (805) 643-5407, (800) 248-2847

The Beneficial Insect Co. — *www.thebeneficialinsectco.com* - P.O. Box 119 Glendale Springs, NC 282629 (336)-973-8490

Worm's Way, Inc. - *www.wormsway.com* — 3151 South Highway 446, Bloomington, IN 47401, (800) 274-9676

HARMFUL INSECTS
Aphids

Aphids are sucking insects that can destroy the tender growth of plants, causing stunted and curled leaf growth and leaving a honeydew deposit. They can be controlled by strong blasts of water and the release of ladybugs. Garlic-pepper tea sprays are also effective.Protecting ladybugs and lacewings and promoting soil health and biodiversity is the best control for these indicator pests. Regular releases of beneficial insects give excellent control, but adapted plants and healthy soil is the best permanent control.

Ants

There are many different ants, including carpenter ants, fire ants, and pharaoh ants. Solutions for ants indoors include natural diatomaceous earth, boric acid, cinnamon, and baking soda. Fire ant mounds should be treated with the mound drench solution. See formulas on page 159. Treat the site with beneficial nematodes and go organic. The competition of microorganisms, insects, lizards, frogs, toads, birds, and even plants is not enjoyed by fire ants. Control carpenter and other house ants with sweet baits that contain small amounts of boric acid. Orange oil or d-limonene sprays will also kill them. Abamectin baits are needed for recurring problems.

Bagworms

Bagworms are common pests of ornamental trees and some shrubs. They will prey on many different species of plants such as cedar, juniper, cypress, etc. In the larval stage, they can defoliate trees. They can be controlled with *Bacillus thuringiensis* (Bt) in the spring. Hand picking the bags is the only control once the bags have been attached to the plants. Trichogramma wasps can also help to control problem infestations.

Bees

Bees are beneficial and should be protected. For the proper environmental control, contact the beekeeper club or society in your area. They will usually come and get them or give you advice on control. Problem bees can be killed with soapy water. Toxic poisons should never be used, especially to kill out colonies. Other insects forage the poisoned honey late in the season and kill out their own colonies. Pollinator insect populations are seriously on the decline because of the use of toxic chemical pesticides.

Beetles

Many adult beetles eat plant foliage and can destroy plants completely. An effective solution for destructive beetles is dry natural diatomaceous earth followed by a spray of Garrett Juice plus orange oil at two ounces per gallon of spray. Garlic tea is an even less toxic control. It's important to remember that many beetles are beneficial, only eat problem insects, and should be protected.

Borers

Borers attack sick softwood trees and various other trees that are in stress. Adult beetles will eat tender terminal growth and then deposit their eggs in the base of the tree. Eggs hatch into larvae and bore into trees and tunnel through the wood until the tree is weakened. Active, tunneling larvae can be killed with a stiff wire run into the holes. Orange oil painted on trunks or injected into holes will also kill them. Beneficial nematodes applied directly in holes will usually kill active larvae, but keeping trees healthy and out of stress is the best prevention. A generous amount of diatomaceous earth at the base of susceptible trees will also help. Applying beneficial nematodes to the soil is also effective. Tree Goop is also helpful.

Cabbage Loopers

Cabbage loopers are caterpillars. They are the larvae of moths that are brown with silver spots in the middle of each wing. They can be killed with *Bacillus thuringiensis* (Bt) spray when the insects are young. Add an ounce of molasses per gallon of spray. Spray late in the day since these guys feed at night. Trichogramma wasps will also help control these critters. It's interesting that even the chemical "pushers" admit that the chemical insecticides are ineffective at controlling loopers.

Cankerworms

Cankerworms (also caterpillars) hang on silk threads from trees. They do a lot of damage to foliage. Wasps will usually control them. If not, spray *Bacillus thuringiensis* (Bt) or the fire ant drench mix for heavy infestations. Release trichogramma wasps in spring.

Chiggers

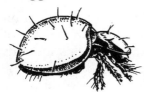

Chiggers are known for their very annoying bites. The itching usually starts the day after you are bitten and lasts two to four days. Natural diatomaceous earth and light applications of sulfur control the critters. Vinegar or orange oil rubbed on bites will eliminate the itching.

Chinch Bugs

Chinch bugs are tiny, black and white, pinhead-size or smaller bugs. During hot, dry weather, chinch bugs can destroy unhealthy lawns. The lawns will look yellow, turn brown, and then die. A dusting of natural diatomaceous earth works in the hot dry weather, also Garrett Juice plus orange oil. This insect hardly ever attacks healthy, well-maintained grass.

Crickets

Crickets live in and out of doors, destroy fabrics such as wool, cotton, synthetics, and silk, and also attack plants. Their irritating sound is the primary objection, although they will eat tender sprouts of wildflowers and vegetables. Solutions outdoors include natural diatomaceous earth, and boric acid for indoor use. *Nosema locustae* is a biological bait for overall control. Orange oil sprays will also kill them effectively.

Elm Leaf Beetles

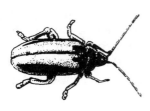

Wherever there is an American, Siberian, or cedar elm tree, elm leaf beetles can be found. They will eat and damage foliage and then move to the next tree. Trees can die from defoliation, but only unhealthy trees are seriously attacked by elm leaf beetles. Solutions include spinosad, plant oil products, and *Bacillus thuringiensis* (Bt). Strong populations of beneficial insects will also help.

Fire Ants

Spray the infested site with one of the plant oil products or Garrett Juice plus two ounces of orange oil per gallon of water. Drench mounds and apply beneficial nematodes to the site.

Then, go organic. The biodiversity of microbes, insects, and other animals is the best long term control. Spraying the site regularly with compost tea or Garrett Juice is also helpful. Grapefruit and orange peelings ground up into a pulp can be on fire ant mounds to help with control. Spinosad products also work.

Fire Ant Drench Formula — mix one part compost tea, one part molasses, and one part orange oil or d-limonene concentrate. Use four to six ounces of concentrate per gallon of water for treating fire ant mounds.

> **Three Simple Steps Fire Ant Program**
> Treat site and drench mounds with
> orange oil products.
> Release beneficial nematodes.
> Go organic.

Fleas

For the control of fleas and ticks apply the following:

1. Spray the infested site with fire ant drench formula. See formulas on page 159.

2. Treat the site with beneficial nematodes. These are living organisms so use before the date deadline on the package.

3. Dust pet sleeping quarters, if necessary, with natural diatomaceous earth. Bathe pets with mild herbal shampoos. The most effective products contain orange oil (d-limonene) and tea tree oil (melaleuca). Citrus products may burn cats' skin.

4. Spray the site regularly with Garrett Juice or aerated compost tea.

Flies

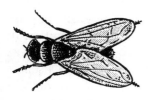

Flies can be repelled with fresh, crushed tansy or garlic. They can also be killed with fly swatters. On the farm, they can be greatly reduced by feeding the animals natural diatomaceous earth daily at two percent of their ratios. Fly parasites are an economical and most effective control. Hanging clear bags of water is another effective control.

Flea Hoppers

These are common vegetable-garden pests that suck juices from the foliage and causes a loss of leaf color that stresses plants. Sulfur (light applications) and natural diatomaceous earth will help. Plant oil sprays are also effective.

Forest Tent Caterpillars

These caterpillars will sometimes do some damage in early spring and early summer, but, if pesticides are avoided, the beneficial wasps will usually keep these guys under control. *Bacillus thuringiensis* (Bt) can be  used if they get out of hand. At worst, they are only a temporary problem. They can also be killed with the fire ant mound drench mix. Release trichogramma wasps in the spring.

Fungus Gnats

Fungus gnats are present when the soil surface is too wet. They can also come in on bananas. They do little, if any, damage but are annoying. They can be gotten rid of by drying out the soil. Baking soda sprayed lightly on soil will quickly solve the problem. A neem drench is also effective. Orange oil spray kills them on contact. Traps can be made by putting a small amount of apple cider vinegar in a bowl with two drops of liquid soap.

Grasshoppers

Do not mow or spray the grasses and weeds under fence lines. Females need bare soil to lay their eggs. Spray *Garrett Juice* mixed with two ounces of orange oil per gallon. Add one quart of kaolin clay per two gallons of water with one tablespoon of Plant Wash. Adding garlic-pepper tea to the mix also helps. Dust the plants with all-purpose flour, which forms glue as the insects try to feed. Go organic. Plant a strongly biodiverse garden and landscape. In other words, use lots of different plants and, yes, encourage the various insect eating animals. A biological bait, *Nosema locustae,* is also available and helpful with the overall program. When the humidity is low, dust plants with natural diatomaceous earth. Cover all bare soil with mulch and feed the birds regularly.

Grubworms

Grubworms are the larvae of June bugs. The adult beetles will chew some leaves and the grubs will eat the roots of grass and garden plants. Not all grubs are harmful; in fact only about 10 percent of the species eat plant roots. The other 90 percent eat decaying organic matter, aerate the soil, and are beneficial. Control of the bad guys comes from being organic and having healthy soil with lots of beneficial organisms and other insects. To speed up the control, apply beneficial nematodes and molasses at ten to twenty pounds per thousand square feet.

Lacebugs

Lacebugs attack various deciduous trees and broad-leafed evergreens. Lacebugs are flat and oval and suck the sap from the underside of the leaf. A quick solution for these pests is garlic-pepper tea and natural diatomaceous earth. Healthy biodiversity in the garden will eliminate destructive population of this pest. Garrett Juice plus orange oil will also help. Use Plant Wash as a helpful surfactant.

Leafhoppers

Leafhoppers damage plants with their piercing and sucking mouth parts and excrete honeydew, causing stunted, dwarfed, and yellow foliage. They can be controlled with a mix of Garrett Juice and garlic tea or simply by the encouragement of diverse populations of beneficial insects.

Leaf Miners

Leaf miners tunnel through leaf tissue and cause brown foliage tips that can spread over the entire leaf. Neem products are effective. Garrett Juice with garlic tea will help. They cause minor damage only, so treatment is rarely needed.

Leaf Skeletonizers

These insect larvae are sawflies. They do cosmetic damage to red oak and other tree leaves. It's rarely necessary to treat. Damage is usually confined to isolated spots in the foliage. Plant oil products are effective.

Mealybugs

Mealybugs are sucking insects that look like cotton on plant stems. Mealybugs suck sap from the foliage and stems and can destroy plants.

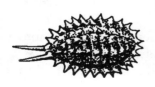

Mealybugs like warm weather and also infest houseplants. Helpful controls include soap and water, predator insects, natural diatomaceous earth, and lizards. For houseplant problems, dab alcohol on bugs with a cotton swab. The fire ant mound drench used as a spray will also work.

Mosquitoes

Mosquitoes are easier to control with organic techniques than with toxic chemicals. Here's the plan.

1. Empty standing water where possible.

2. Treat water that cannot be emptied with gambusia fish or Bti (*Bacillus thuringiensis* 'Israelensis') product such as Bactimos Briquettes or Mosquito Dunks.

3. Spray for adult mosquitoes with plant oil products.

4. Use organic management to encourage birds, bats, dragonflies, and other beneficial insects.

5. Use skin repellents that contain natural herbs such as aloe vera, citronella, vanilla, eucalyptus, tea tree oil, and citrus oil. Do not use DEET products. It is far too toxic, especially for children.

6. Bug zapping light devices do not work! Not unless you chain your dog to the device to provide the carbon dioxide. Mosquitoes are attracted to living organisms, not cold machines.

7. Broadcast dry granulated garlic to the problem areas.

Nematodes

Many nematodes are beneficial, but there are those that will attack ornamental trees, garden plants, and lawn grass. Controls include increasing the organic level in soil, using organic fertilizers, and applying products that increase microbial activity. Cedar flakes applied to the soil surface will also help. Citrus pulp tilled into the soil prior to planting is an excellent preventative.

Pill Bugs

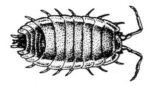

Pill bugs, or sow bugs, or roly-poly bugs are crustaceans and are related to shrimp, crabs, and crawfish. They are found in damp places and feed on organic matter but when abundant will also eat plants. Beer in a trap is still one solution, but not a very good one.

Banana peels attract them so you can scoop them up and drop into a soapy water solution. A mix of cedar flakes, hot pepper, and natural diatomaceous earth is effective. Mulch using shredded cedar. Spray plant oil products or spinosad.

Plum Curculios

The larvae of these insects bore into fruit. See the Fruit and Pecan Program in the appendix. Make sure the root flares of the trees are exposed. Regular spraying of garlic tea is one the best organic preventatives. Biodiversity is critical for control of this pest. Spray foliage biweekly with Garrett Juice plus garlic tea.

Roaches

There are numerous cockroaches, but only a few really pose a problem. Cockroaches usually live outdoors and are nocturnal by nature. Roaches will enter a home or building through any crack or crevice. Roaches will chew on cloth or books. Solutions include: a shoe, newspaper, natural diatomaceous earth, keeping your house clean, eliminating drips, leaks and standing water, and sealing all openings. A light dusting of boric acid or natural diatomaceous earth indoors gives effective control. Spray orange oil products. See the appendix for bait formulas.

Scale

Scale insects attach to stems, branches, and trunks and suck sap from the plants. Controls include horticultural oil and plant oil products. Use Plant Wash and water with a mild orange spray on interior plants. The black, scale-eating ladybug feeds on scale insects outdoors.

Slugs

Slugs and snails must be kept moist at all times and will go anywhere there is moisture. Effective controls include garlic-pepper tea, natural diatomaceous earth, and wood ashes. They can also be repelled with a mix of natural diatomaceous earth, hot pepper, and cedar flakes. The commercial product Sluggo is also effective.

Squash Bugs

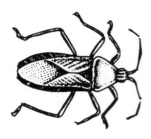

Squash bugs are difficult-to-control insects that attack squash, cucumbers, pumpkins, and other cucurbits. Control by smashing the eggs, dusting the adults with natural diatomaceous earth, and planting lemon balm in between plants. Dusting young plants regularly with cheap self-rising flour will also help. Treat soil with beneficial nematodes and spray with Garrett Juice plus orange oil. Planting a larger number of squash plants also seems to help.

Squash Vine Borers

The squash vine borers are insects whose larvae are worms that bore into the base stem of squash, cucumber, melon, gourd, and pumpkin. Cut the stem open, remove the worms, and cover the wounded area with Tree Goop. Another way is to inject Bt into the base of the stem with a syringe. Spraying with Bt will also help. Treat soil with beneficial nematodes.

Spider Mites

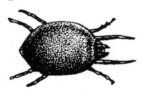

Red spider mites or just spider mites are very small spider kinfolks and feed on garden plants and ornamental trees. You probably will not see the mites at first, but you will notice the webbing that accompanies them. The best control is beneficial insects such as green lacewings. Controls also include spraying Garrett Juice plus garlic and extra seaweed. Seaweed spray by itself also works. Strong blasts of water or soapy water are good for small infestations. Predatory mites are also effective.

Stink Bugs

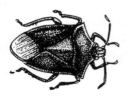

Stink bugs punch holes in foliage and fruit and cause rotted spots. Some stink bugs, on the other hand, are beneficial. The pest ones can be controlled with a spray of Garrett Juice plus orange oil or a dusting of natural diatomaceous earth.

Termites

Treat all exposed wood with borate products such as Tim-Bor or Bora-Care or hot pepper. Inject these same products by foam into the walls. Use 00 sandblasting sand (also sold as 16 grit sand) as a physical barrier in leave-outs in slabs, against the edge of slabs, and on both sides of beams. New construction can use it under slabs. Treat the soil around the structure with beneficial nematodes. Ignore the nuts that say to remove the mulch from around the house. There is a commercial product called Bio-Blast which is a beneficial fungus product.

Thrips

Thrips attack buds and tight-petaled flowers such as roses, mums, and peonies. Thrips are not visible to the naked eye, but will rasp the plant tissue and drain the sap. Heavy infestations can kill plants. Thrips are general eaters and will attack flowers or field crops. Controls include spraying Garrett Juice plus garlic and releasing green lacewings. Biweekly spraying of Garrett Juice is all that is usually needed long term. Apply beneficial nematodes to the soil before bud break in the early spring.

Ticks

Ticks are difficult to control, but dusting with natural diatomaceous earth and using the flea program will control these pests (see page 103). Bathing the pets regularly with herbal ingredients will help considerably.

Whiteflies

Whiteflies are very small and resemble little white moths. Whiteflies are extremely hard to control with chemicals and will suck the juices from several kinds of plants. They will attack vegetables and ornamental plants outdoors and indoors; however, beneficial insect populations will prevent the pest. Whiteflies have many natural enemies. Spray Garrett Juice plus orange oil, seaweed plus garlic-pepper tea or spinosad.

The Organic Manual

ORGANIC PEST REMEDY OPTIONS

APHIDS

Controls	Application
Water blast	Use hose nozzle or a strong thumb.
Garlic-pepper tea	Spray as needed.
Beneficial insects	Release ladybugs, braconid wasps, and green lacewings until a balanced population of bugs exists.

ANTS (Fire Ants, Carpenter Ants, and Pharoah Ants [Sugar])

Controls	Application
Mound Drench	Mix of sugar and boric acid (for indoor use only).
Boric acid and sugar	Use in bait stations (indoors only).
Garrett Juice	Add 2 oz. of orange oil or d-limonene per gal. of water.
Tansy	Sprinkle bits of tansy leaf in problem area.
Baking soda	Dust indoors to control sugar ants.
Cinnamon	Dust indoors and on fire ants.

BAGWORMS, CATERPILLARS, CORN BORERS, CABBAGEWORMS, ARMYWORMS

Controls	Application
Bt (*Bacillus thuringiensis*)	Spray with 1 oz. liquid molasses per gal. at dusk.
Beneficial insects	Encourage and protect native wasps. Release green lacewings and trichogramma wasps.
Orange oil	Spray as needed at 2 oz. per gal. of water.

BEETLES (Elm leaf beetle, Flea beetle, and Borer beetle)

Controls	Application
Spinosad products	Make sure beetle in question is harmful—many are beneficial. Encourage biodiversity of insects, birds, plants, and small animals.
Neem	Use all per label instructions.
Citrus products	Use all per label instructions.

BORERS, TREE

Controls	Application
Orange oil	Use 4–6 oz. per gallon of water (on trunk only).
Nematodes	Put into holes full strength and moisten. Also treat the root zone per label directions.
Tree Goop	Apply to tree trunks as necessary.

CASEBEARERS

Controls	Application
Trichogramma wasp	Release eggs at least every 2 weeks starting with leaf emergence, usually mid-March.
Bt (*Bacillus thuringiensis*)	Spray with 1 oz. molasses per gal. at dusk.

110

Organic Pest Remedies (continued)

CRICKETS, CHIGGERS, CHINCH BUGS

Controls	Application
Natural diatomaceous earth	Dust infested area @ 1 cup per 1,000 sq. ft.
Garrett Juice plus orange oil	Add 2 oz. of orange oil concentrate per gal. of spray.
Nosema locustae (crickets - outside)	Broadcast on infested area.
Dusting sulfur (outside use)	Dust on legs to prevent chigger bites.

COLORADO POTATO BUG

Controls	Application
Bt 'San Diego'	Spray late in the day per label instructions.
Garlic-pepper tea	Spray liquid mix as needed.
Natural diatomaceous earth	Dust plants as needed.

CUTWORMS

Controls	Application
Natural diatomaceous earth	Pour a ring of material around each plant.
Bone meal	Pour a ring of material around each plant.
Bt (*Bacillus thuringiensis*)	Apply per label at dusk. Add 1 tsp. liquid soap per gal.
Collars	Wrap aluminum foil around veggie stem.
Beneficial nematodes	Apply to the soil prior to planting.
Spinosad products	Spray as needed.

ELM LEAF BEETLE

Controls	Application
Horticulture oil	Spray per label for severe problems.
Garlic-pepper tea	¼ cup concentrate per gallon.
Bt (*Bacillus thuringiensis*)	Spray per label at dusk. Add 1 oz. of molasses per gal.
Garrett Juice plus orange oil	Add 2 oz. of orange oil concentrate per gal. of spray.

FLIES

Controls	Application
Garlic tea	Spray infested area.
Yellow sticky traps	Hang in infested area.
Tansy	Grind the herb and apply as a dry powder.
Natural diatomaceous earth	Add to livestock and pet food.
Fly parasites	Release as needed.
Bags of clear water	Hang clear plastic bags of water.

FLEA BEETLES

Controls	Application
Garrett Juice plus orange oil	Spray as needed. Add 2 oz. orange oil per gal.
Garlic-pepper tea	Spray at first sign of problem.
Natural diatomaceous earth	Dust as needed.
Spinosad products	Spray as needed.

Organic Pest Remedies (continued)

FLEAS

Controls	Application
Garrett Juice	Spray as needed to stimulate biological activity.
Plant oil products	Follow label instructions.
Orange oil or d-limonene products	Follow label instructions.
Natural diatomaceous earth	Dust infested areas.
Bathing	Bathe pets regularly in mild soapy water. Herbal shampoos are best.
Beneficial nematodes	Apply to soil per label directions. Critical step.

FUNGUS GNATS

Controls	Application
Neem products	Apply per label instructions, drench soil.
Water schedule	Allow soil to dry out between waterings.
Orange oil spray	Spray the adults for a contact kill.

GRASSHOPPERS

Controls	Application
Nosema locustae products	Broadcast per label instructions when grasshoppers are young.
Hot pepper spray	Blast them as needed. Add garlic and citrus oil for more power.
Kaoline clay	Mix and spray with water and 1 tsp. per gal. of Plant Wash.
Biodiversity	Plant heavily and use many species.
Birds	Feed, water, and attract as many as possible.

GRUBWORMS

Controls	Application
Beneficial nematodes	Release per label instructions.
Sugar or dry molasses	Broadcast @ 5–10 lbs. per 1,000 sq.ft.
Compost tea	Spray and drench soil.

LACEBUGS

Controls	Application
Garlic-pepper tea	Spray liquid mix as needed.
Garrett Juice plus garlic tea	Add citrus oil for more power.
Horticultural oil	Per label instructions.
Beneficial insects	Release praying mantises and ladybugs as necessary.

LEAFHOPPERS

Controls	Application
Garlic-pepper tea plus natural diatomaceous earth	Add the DE at 1 cup per gallon of spray.
Garrett Juice plus garlic tea	Add citrus oil for additional power.
Praying mantises	Release as necessary.

Organic Pest Remedies (continued)

LEAFMINERS

Controls	Application
Neem	Spray per label instructions.
Don't worry about 'em	Minor damage only, usually no need to treat.
Spray Garrett Juice plus garlic tea	Omit the garlic once the infestation is reduced.

LOOPERS

Controls	Application
Bt (*Bacillus thuringiensis*)	Apply per label instructions at dusk.
Beneficial insects	Release regularly until healthy, native populations exist. Trichogramma wasps are the most effective.

MEALYBUGS

Controls	Application
Horticulture oil	Apply per label instructions. Add 1 tablespoon molasses per gallon of spray.
Mealybug predators	Release as needed
Lizards	Protect native ones and introduce new ones.
Mound Drench formula	Spray as needed.

MITES

Controls	Application
Garrett Juice plus garlic	Spray as needed.
Seaweed spray	Spray as needed.

MOSQUITOES

Controls	Application
Bti (*Bacillus thuringiensis* 'Israelensis')	Put briquettes or granules in standing water.
Encourage frogs, birds, bats	Eliminate standing, stagnant water.
Instant coffee	Sprinkle crystals in standing water.
Garlic oil	Apply to standing water.
Gambusia and goldfish	Small fish that love the taste of mosquitoe larvae.
Garlic-pepper tea	Spray for adult mosquitoes.
Citronella products	Spray as needed and use candles.
Dry granulated garlic	Broadcast at 2 lbs. per 1000 sq. ft.

MOTHS

Controls	Application
Bt (*Bacillus thuringiensis*)	Spray per label instructions at dusk. Add 1 oz. molasses per gallon.
Beneficial insects	Release ladybugs and green lacewings every two weeks until natural control exists.

Organic Pest Remedies (continued)

NEMATODES (Root Knot and Other Pest Types)

Controls	Application
Compost	Stimulate soil biology with compost, organic fertilizers, and microbe stimulators.
Molasses	Apply dry material at 10 lbs. per 1,000 sq. ft.
Citrus	Apply orange and grapefruit pulp to soil prior to planting.

PECAN CASE BEARER

Controls	Application
Trichogramma wasps	Release every week during the spring. Start at leaf emergence.
Green lacewings	Release as foliage starts to grow.
Bt (*Bacillus thuringiensis*)	Spray in early May. Add 1 oz. molasses per gallon of spray.

PILL BUGS (and Sow Bugs)

Controls	Application
Brewer's yeast and water traps	1 tbs. of yeast per gallon of water.
Bone meal or rock phosphate	Pour a ring around each plant.
Natural diatomaceous earth or wood ashes	Pour a ring around each plant.
Cedar flakes, hot pepper, natural DE	Dust around infested plants.

PLUM CURCULIO

Controls	Application
Garrett Juice plus garlic tea	Spray at pink bud, again after flowers have fallen.
Garlic-pepper tea	Spray during petal fall.
Mulch the tree's root system	Compost, shredded tree trimmings or alfalfa hay.
Tree Goop	Apply to tree trunks on injured limbs as needed.
Dry granulated garlic	Broadcast on the root zone.

ROACHES

Controls	Application
Natural diatomaceous earth	Dust infested area lightly.
Boric acid	Dust infested areas lightly (indoors only).
Boric balls	Boric acid, flour, and sugar. Add water and roll into balls. Use indoors only.
Sugar and baking-soda detergent traps	1–2 tablespoons per bait station. See appendix.
Eliminate food sources	Remove food and water sources daily.
Orange oil products	Spray as needed.

Organic Pest Remedies (continued)

SCALE

Controls	Application
Horticultural oil	Spray per label instructions.
Beneficial insects	Release ladybugs and praying mantises.
Plant Wash	Spray as needed.

SQUASH BUGS

Controls	Application
Mound Drench formula	Spray per label on serious infestations.
Hand removal	Destroy copper colored eggs from the back side of leaves.
Bee balm (lemon balm)	Interplant with veggies.
Natural diatomaceous earth	Dust as needed.
Beneficial nematodes	Treat soil per label directions.

SQUASH VINE BORER

Controls	Application
Bt (*Bacillus thuringiensis*)	Spray very young plants and inject product into stem with syringe.
Beneficial insects	Release trichogramma wasps and green lacewings.
Beneficial nematodes	Treat soil per label instructions.
Plant Wash plus neem	Spray as needed.

STINK BUGS

Controls	Application
Garrett Juice plus garlic tea	Spray per label instructions as needed.
Garlic-pepper tea/diatomaceous earth	Add natural DE to mix at 1 cup per gallon of water.
Plant Wash plus neem	Spray as needed.

SLUGS, SNAILS

Controls	Application
Beer or brewer's yeast traps	Plastic jar or dish sunk into ground.
Garlic-pepper tea and natural diatomaceous earth	Spray as needed.
Natural diatomaceous earth	Dust infested area.
Bone meal or rock phosphate	Dust infested area or put ring around individual plants.
Encourage turtles	The real life kind.
Cedar flakes, natural DE, and hot pepper	Dust around plants as necessary.

Organic Pest Remedies (continued)

SPIDERS

Controls	Application
Physically remove	No need to control spiders except black widow and brown recluse. The others are beneficial.
Orange oil products	Spray orange oil or d-limonene products per label directions.

SOW BUGS (See Pill Bugs)

SPIDER MITES

Controls	Application
Beneficial insects	Release green lacewings and predatory mites.
Liquid seaweed	2 tbs. per gal. Add orange oil for extra effect.
Garlic-pepper tea	Spray every 3 days for 9 days.
Horticultural oil	Per label instructions. Last resort only.
Garrett Juice plus garlic tea	Spray as needed.

TERMITES

Controls	Application
Boric acid	Follow label instructions for indoor use.
Beneficial nematodes	Apply to soil as preventative.
Orange oil products	Spray on active infestations.
Natural diatomaceous earth	Dust as needed.

TICKS

Controls	Application
Natural diatomaceous earth	2 tbs. per gal. Spray or dust infected area.
Garlic-pepper tea	Spray infected area.
Orange oil	Spray infected area as needed.
Beneficial nematodes	Apply to soil per label directions.

THRIPS

Controls	Application
Beneficial insects	Release green lacewings as needed.
Garlic-pepper tea	Spray every 2 weeks or as needed.
Garrett Juice plus garlic tea	Spray as needed. Add Plant Wash to mix.
Beneficial nematodes	Apply to soil before spring buds form.

TOBACCO HORN WORM

Controls	Application
Bt (*Bacillus thuringiensis*)	Spray per label instructions at dusk.
Beneficial insects	Release trichogramma and braconid wasps every 2 weeks.
Hand removal	There are usually only a few.

Organic Pest Remedies (continued)

TOMATO PIN WORM

Controls	Application
Garlic-pepper tea	Spray every 2 weeks.
Garrett Juice plus garlic	Spray as needed.

TREEHOPPERS

Controls	Application
Garrett Juice plus garlic tea	Spray as needed.
Garlic-pepper tea	Spray every 2 weeks or as needed.

WASPS

Controls	Application
Water blast (Protect if possible)	Nests can be moved to new location and nailed in place after spraying wasps with water. Do not attempt if allergic to wasps.
Orange oil products	Spray to repel, not to kill.
Citronella products	Use per label directions

WHITEFLIES

Controls	Application
Yellow sticky traps	Hang in infested area.
Beneficial insects	Release until natural populations exist.
Garrett Juice plus garlic tea	Spray as needed.

WEBWORMS

Controls	Application
Bt (*Bacillus thuringiensis*)	Spray with 1 oz. of molasses per gal. at dusk.
Wasps	Introduce and protect trichogramma wasps and natives.
Mound Drench formula	Spray as needed. Add Plant Wash to mix.

Note: Never apply orange oil or other citrus products at rates stronger than 2 ounces per gallon of water.

ORGANIC DISEASE CONTROL

Disease control in an organic program is easy. Increased resistance to most diseases results as a nice side benefit from the basic organic program.

All organic products help control disease to some degree. When soil and plants are healthy, there is a never-ending microscopic war being waged between the good and bad microorganisms, and the good guys win. Disease problems are simply situations where the microorganisms have gotten out of balance.

Drainage is a key ingredient for the prevention of diseases. Beds or tree pits that hold water and don't drain properly are the ideal breeding place for many disease organisms.

As with insects, spraying toxic chemcials for diseases is only treating symptoms, not the major problems—plus the toxic sprays kill more beneficials than the targeted pests. The primary cause of problems is usually related to the soil and the root system. Therefore it is critical to improve drainage, increase air circulation, add quality composted products, and stimulate and protect the living organisms in the soil.

Anthracnose: A mostly cosmetic fungal problem in sycamore trees, beans, and ornamentals where the foliage turns a tan color. Control is by avoiding susceptible plants. Compost tea, sprayed as leaves emerge in the spring, will sometimes help. Best cure is soil improvement. Treat the soil with the overall Sick Tree Treatment. Spray with hydrogen peroxide or Plant Wash as a cure.

Bacterial Blight: A bacterial disease that causes dark-green water spots that turn brown and may die leaving a hole in the leaves of tomatoes, plums, and several ornamental plants. Controls include healthy soil, garlic tea, hydrogen peroxide and Plant Wash.

Black Spot: Common name of fungal leaf spot that attacks the foliage of plants such as roses. There is usually a yellow halo around the dark spot. Entire leaves then turn yellow and ultimately die. Controls include selection of resistant plants and Garrett Juice plus garlic tea and skim milk. Apply cornmeal to the soil or cornmeal juice to the foliage. Plant Wash is my favorite commercial product. It works great!

Brown Patch: Cool-weather, fungal disease of St. Augustine. Brown leaves pull loose easily from the runners. Small spots in lawn grow into large circles that look bad and weaken the turf, but rarely kill the grass. Soil health, drainage, and low nitrogen input are the best preventatives. Treat diseased turf with cornmeal at ten to twenty pounds per thousand square feet or dry granulated garlic at two pounds per thousand square feet. Spray Garrett Juice with Plant Wash added.

Canker: A stress related disease of trees and shrubs that causes decay of the bark and wood or the formation of clumpy growths. Healthy soil and plants with strong immune systems are the solutions. Apply the Sick Tree Treatment.

Cotton Root Rot: A fungal disease common in alkaline soils that attacks poorly adapted plants. The best preventative is healthy soil with a balance of nutrients and soil biology. Solutions include adding sulfur and sometimes sodium to the soil. Treat the soil with cornmeal at ten to twenty pounds per thousand square feet.

Damping Off: A fungal disease of emerging seedlings where tiny plants fall over as if severed at the ground line. Avoid by using living (not sterilized) potting soil and by placing rock phosphate on the surface of planting media. Treat the soil with cornmeal and spray with Plant Wash.

Entomosporium: A fungal leaf spot disease of photinia, Indian hawthorn, and other plants. It can be controlled by improving soil conditions and avoiding susceptible plants. This disease's real cause is a weak root system. Treat the plants with the Sick Tree Treatment in appendix.

Fireblight: Bacterial disease of plants in the rose family where twigs and limbs die back as though they've been burned. Leaves usually remain attached, but often turn black or dark brown. Prune back into healthy tissue and disinfect pruning tools with 3 percent solution of hydrogen peroxide. Spray plants at first sign of disease with hydrogen peroxide or Plant Wash. Treat plants with the Sick Tree Treatment and cut back on the amount of nitrogen fertilizer.

Gray Leaf Spot: A disease of St. Augustine grass that forms gray vertical spots on the grass blades. A light baking-soda or potassium bicarbonate spray is the best curative. Prevent by improving soil health. Treat the soil with cornmeal at ten to twenty pounds per thousand square feet. Plant Wash is also effective.

Oak Wilt: A disease of the vascular system of oak trees that is transmitted through the air by insects and through the root system of neighboring trees by natural grafting. Biodiversity and soil health are the best deterrents. See the Sick Tree Treatment in the appendix. I do not recommend injecting toxic chemical fungicides into the tree. That only treats symptoms.

Powdery Mildew: White or gray, powdery, fungal growth on the leaf surface and flower buds of zinnias, crape myrtles, and many vegetables. Best control is Plant Wash and the Sick Tree Treatment.

Sooty Mold: Black fungal growth on the foliage of gardenias, crape myrtles, and other plants infested with aphids, scale, or whiteflies. It is caused by the honeydew (poop) of the insect pests. Best control is to release beneficial insects to control the pest bugs. Spray with Garrett Juice plus garlic tea or orange oil and Plant Wash.

St. Augustine Decline: Virus in common St. Augustine grass that causes a yellow mottling. The grass slowly dies away. The answer is to replace turf with a healthier grass. The best St. Augustine at the moment is "Raleigh." Switching to the organic program will eliminate the problem in most cases. Plant Wash spray will help.

ORGANIC DISEASE CONTROL

ANTHRACNOSE

Controls	Application
Potassium bicarbonate	Spray emerging foliage at 4 teaspoons per gal.
Better soil health	Use mulch, compost, rock powders, biostimulants.
Sick Tree Treatment	See appendix.
Plant Wash	Spray as needed.

BACTERIAL BLIGHT

Controls	Application
Hydrogen peroxide	Spray as needed mixed with Garrett Juice.
Garlic-pepper tea	Spray as needed per label instructions.
Better soil health	Use mulch, compost, rock powders, and biostimulants.
Garrett Juice plus garlic tea	Spray as needed.
Plant Wash	Spray as needed.

BLACK SPOT (Fungal leaf spot)

Control	Application
Potassium bicarbonate	Spray lightly as needed. Potassium bicarbonate is better.
Better soil health	Use mulch, compost, rock powders, biostimulants.
Garrett Juice plus garlic tea	Add skim milk for even more power.
Cornmeal	Apply to soil at 20 lbs. per 1,000 sq. ft.

Organic Disease Control (continued)

BROWN PATCH

Controls	Application
Horticultural cornmeal	Apply at 10–20 lbs. per 1,000 sq. ft.
Better soil health	Mulch, compost, rock powders, biostimulants. Avoid wet soil and high-nitrogen fertilizers.
Potassium bicarbonate	Spray as needed. Mix with Garrett Juice.
Plant Wash	Spray as needed.

CANKER

Controls	Application
Increase drainage	Change planting site, aerate soil and mulch.
Delay pruning until bud swell	Never make flush cuts or use pruning paint.
Better soil health	Mulch, compost, rock powders, biostimulants. Use the Sick Tree Treatment.

FIREBLIGHT

Controls	Application
Garlic-pepper tea	Spray plants while in bloom.
Better soil health	Mulch, compost, rock powders, biostimulants.
Limit use of nitrogen	Cut off infected area.
Garrett Juice plus garlic	Add Plant Wash for additional power.
Hydrogen peroxide	Can be added to any of the above mixes.

GRAY LEAF SPOT

Controls	Application
Potassium bicarbonate	Light foliage spray as needed.
Better soil health	Aerate and balance the soil nutrients.
Garrett Juice plus garlic tea	Spray as needed.
Cornmeal	Broadcast at 20 lbs. per 1,000 sq. ft.
Plant Wash	Spray as needed.

OAK WILT

Controls	Application
Maintain soil and plant health	Fertilize with organic techniques, and water regularly.
Sick Tree Treatment	See appendix.

POWDER MILDEW

Controls	Application
Baking-soda spray	Light foliage spray as needed. Potassium bicarbonate is better.
Better soil health	Use mulch, compost, rock powders, biostimulants.
Garrett Juice plus garlic	Spray as needed.
Horticultural cornmeal	Broadcast at 20 lbs. per 1,000 sq. ft.
Plant Wash	Spray as needed.

Organic Disease Control (continued)

PEACH TREE CURL

Controls	Application
Baking-soda spray	Spray in fall. Potassium bicarbonate is better.
Garrett Juice plus garlic tea	Spray in fall.
Better soil health	Use mulch, compost, rock powders, and biostimulants.
Sick Tree Treatment	See appendix.

SOOTY MOLD

Controls	Application
Baking-soda spray	Light spray as needed. Potassium bicarbonate is better.
Beneficial insects	Ladybugs and green lacewings will control aphids whose honeydew causes the sooty mold.
Garrett Juice plus garlic tea	Spray as needed.
Plant Wash	Spray as needed.

TAKE-ALL-PATCH

Controls	Application
Horticultural cornmeal	Apply at 20 lbs. per 1,000 sq. ft.
Apple cider vinegar	Spray at 2 oz. per gal.

Note:
Since the first edition, I have gotten smart enough to stop recommending all copper based products. Copper is a heavy metal that is needed in very small amounts in the soil, but can very easily accumulate to toxic levels.

WEEDS

Have you ever read anything good about the weeds? Unless you've read Malcolm Beck's *Lessons in Nature* or Charles Walters' *Weeds*, probably not!

Weeds are nature's greatest and most diverse group of plants. Even though many members of the weed fraternity are beautiful, man has been convinced by the chemical poison fraternity to condemn the weeds and consider them his enemy. Mention weeds and most people think in terms of control through spraying toxic pesticides. They rarely think of why the weeds grow or of their value.

Weeds are here on earth for very specific purposes. Different weeds have different jobs to do. Some are here to provide the soil a green blanket to shade and cool the ground. Others are here to prevent the erosion of bare soil. Others are here to help balance the minerals in the soil. Many weeds provide all these important functions.

Weeds take no chances. They germinate and spread to protect any soil left bare from mismanagement of the land. In every cubic foot of soil lie millions of weed seeds waiting to germinate when needed. When bare soil is exposed, weeds are needed. When hard winters freeze the ornamental lawn grasses, weeds are needed. When we mow too low and apply harsh chemicals to the soil, weeds are needed.

If it weren't for weeds, the topsoil of the earth would have eroded away years ago. Much of the topsoil has already gone from our farms forever to muddy our rivers and fill our lakes and eventually end up in our oceans.

It's a common misunderstanding that weeds rob our crops of moisture, sunlight, and nutrients. Weeds only borrow water and nutrients and eventually return it all to the soil for future crop use.

Weeds are tough. Rarely do you find weeds destroyed by insects or disease. Some weeds are pioneer plants as they are able to grow in soil unsuited for edible or domesticated plants. Weeds are able to build the soil with their strong and powerful roots that go deep, penetrating and loosening hard-packed soil. The deep roots bring minerals, especially trace elements, from the subsoil to the topsoil.

Weeds are indicators of certain soil deficiencies and actually collect or manufacture certain mineral elements that are lacking in the soil. This is nature's wonderful way of buffering and balancing the soil.

Some weeds are good companion plants. Some have insect-repelling abilities, while others with deep roots help surface-feeding plants obtain moisture during dry spells. Weeds act as straws to bring water up from the deep, moist soil so that shallow-rooted plants can get some of the moisture.

Control becomes necessary when the vigorous weeds become too numerous in the fields and gardens. However, not understanding the dangers of spraying toxic chemicals (like RoundUp, 2,4–D, MSMA, etc.) into the environment, farmers, gardeners, and landscape people have primarily used these powerful toxic herbicides. Most herbicides upset the harmony of the soil organisms, and some herbicides can persist in the soil for months or longer. Even though microbes can repopulate after chemical treatment damage, they are slow to reestablish the complicated, natural balance.

There are safe and nonpolluting weed control methods such as mechanically aerating, mulching with organic materials, and using organic fertilizers to stimulate the growth of more desirable plants. The old, reliable methods of hand weeding, hoeing, and timely cultivating are not yet against the law and are good exercise.

The best weed control in turf is the following: Water deeply, but infrequently, fertilize with natural organic fertilizers, mow at a higher setting, and leave the clippings on the ground. Easy and effective weed control in the ornamental and vegetable beds is done by keeping a thick blanket of mulch on the bare soil at all times. Clover, wild violets, and other herbs and wildflowers should sometimes be encouraged. Many plants that start out looking like noxious weeds end up presenting beautiful flower displays and wonderful fragrances. They're called wildflowers.

Weed control starts with a new attitude about weeds. A few are acceptable, even beneficial.

Organic Herbicide

Sometimes, weeds need to be killed, and there are safe alternatives. There are commercial citric acid and fatty acid products on the market, but some gardeners like to make their own. Here is my favorite formula.

> 1 gallon full strength 10 percent vinegar
> 1 ounce orange oil
> 1 tablespoon molasses
> 1 teaspoon Plant Wash or other liquid soap

Vinegar strengths vary. 5 percent is regular vinegar, and doesn't work well for weed control. 10 percent is pickling vinegar. 20 percent is too strong, and I no longer recommend it. If used, avoid contact with skin and breathing the fumes.

Be sure to keep the mix well shaken while spraying. Avoid products that are made from glacial acetic acid. They are petroleum based products.

The commercial product using my formula is the Soil Mender Enhanced Vinegar. Fatty acid products can also be used or mixed with the above formula for greater strength.

ORGANIC WEED CONTROL

WEEDS (general)

Controls	Application
Vinegar products	Spot spray as needed.
Chop with a hoe or hand remove	This is still legal.
Accept a few	Many "weeds" are herbs, wildflowers, and beneficial
Fatty acid products	Spot spray as needed.

BERMUDAGRASS, ST. AUGUSTINE

Controls	Application
Vinegar products	Spray as needed.
Dig out	Use a sod cutter or hoe to remove rhizomes and stolons.
Fatty acid products	Spot spray as needed.

NUTGRASS

Controls	Application
Ryegrass	Overseed turf areas.
Mulch	Cover weeds in beds with a thick blanket of mulch.
Hand remove	Dig out infested area and sift through wire mesh to catch the nutlets and roots.
Chemical products	Avoid like the plague. They injure and kill trees.
Dry molasses	Apply heavy application.

JOHNSONGRASS

Controls	Application
Physically remove	Can't stand to be mowed or regularly cut down.

CRABGRASS

Controls	Application
Fertilizer	Crabgrass can't stand fertility.
Mowing height	Mow at a height of 3" or more.
Vinegar products	Spray as needed.
Cinnamon products	Apply per label directions.

DALLISGRASS

Controls	Application
Cornmeal	Apply ¼" over the entire weed and water. Molasses also works to rot the crown. Dig out later.
Physical removal	Dig out with mechanical tools.
Vinegar/citrus products	Spray prior to physical removal.
MSMA?	This toxic product recommended by organiphobes is far too toxic. The "A" stands for arsenic.

Organic Weed Control (continued)

POISON IVY

Controls	Application
Physically remove plants	Do not attempt if you are highly allergic. Protect skin.
Vinegar products	Spray young growth as it emerges.
Comfrey juice	Apply to skin to prevent or to relieve rash pain.

POND ALGAE

Controls	Application
Tilapia fish*	Release in spring after water temperature is above 60°.
Water circulation	Circulating water with pump or fountain.
Cornmeal	Broadcast across water surface at 5 lbs. per 1,000 sq. ft. 150 lbs. per surface acre.

POND WEEDS

Organic Solution	Application
White amur fish*	Release in spring after water temperature is above 60°.

*License for both these fish available through fish and wildlife departments.

MISCELLANEOUS ORGANIC CONTROL

STUPID NEIGHBORS

Control	Application
Try to help them or move	Give them the names of organic books to read; ask them to www.dirtdoctor.com and read "The Natural Way" in The *Dallas Morning News* on Friday.

ALLERGIES

Control	Application
Mint and honey tea	10 cups of water, 5 sprigs spearmint, 2 applemint, 2 bee balm, 1 peppermint, 1 tablespoon honey, and a slice of lemon. Steep—don't boil, drink, and enjoy.
Exercise	Do exercises and yoga positions where the head is lower than the body

ORGANIC ANIMAL CONTROL

ARMADILLOS

Control	Application
Live traps	Need to use batter boards to form a "V" to guide them into the trap.
Hot pepper	Broadcasting hot pepper can sometimes work.

BIRDS

Control	Application
Cats	I'd rather have the birds.
Soapy water	Last resort: spray roosting birds with mild liquid soap solution. Do in warm weather only.
Garlic-pepper spray	Most birds are beneficial and a natural mix of life in the garden will usually control populations.

CATS

Control	Application
Dogs	Or keep the cats indoors.
Citrus extract or peelings	Apply to problem areas.
Live traps	Use as needed.
Dry cayenne or other hot pepper	Spread around problem area.
Rose cuttings	Spread any thorny cuttings in beds.
Citronella	Spray as needed.
Lava gravel	Use as a mulch.

DEER

Control	Application
Deer Scram™	Apply per label directions.
Soap bar	Hang in trees in problem areas.
Blood meal	Spread around problem areas.
Human hair	Put in porous bags.
Commercial repellants	Apply per label directions.

DOGS

Control	Application
Live traps	Use as needed.
Dog runs	It is not cruel to house dogs in dog runs when not at home.
Dog-B-Gone	1 part cayenne pepper, 2 parts mustard powder, 2 parts flour, or use straight cayenne or other hot pepper.
Hot pepper	Dust as needed.

Organic Animal Control (continued)

GOPHERS

Control	Application
Black Hole Gopher Trap™	Install in tunnel per instructions.
Gopher spurge	Plant gopher spurge (*Euphobia lathyrus*) around the perimeter of problem area.
Caster bean plants	Plant as a barrier to garden areas.
Garlic	Plant as a barrier to garden areas.
Other metal traps	Install in tunnels per instructions.
Hot pepper-castor oil	Inject in the problem areas and spray on surface.
Noisy devices	Install windmills or rattling devices.

MICE

Control	Application
Cats	Hope you aren't allergic.
Traps	Still looking for a better one.
Baits	Apply in bait stations.
Hot pepper	Dust dry material.
Peppermint	Use ground-up pieces of mint or cardboard soaked in peppermint oil as repellent.
Fox urine	Apply per label directions.

MOLES

Control	Application
Same as for gophers	At least you have nice, sandy soil.

RABBITS

Control	Application
Low and recessed fences	Electric fences are even better.
Cayenne or other pepper	Dust onto problem area.
Blood meal	Spread around problem area.
Fox urine	Apply per label directions.
Commercial repellants	Apply per label directions.
Rabbit Scram™	Apply per label directions.

RACCOONS

Control	Application
Live traps	Use as needed.
Garlic-pepper tea	Spray as needed.

RATS

Control	Application
Death traps	Still looking for a better one.
Live traps	Use as needed.
Bait stations	Rampage or Quintox per label directions.
Fox urine	Apply as needed.

Pest Control

Organic Animal Control (continued)

SKUNKS

Control	Application
Live traps	Use as needed.
	Be careful of the spray and bites. Many skunks are rabid.
Fox urine	Apply as needed.

SNAKES

Control	Application
Introduce bull and king snakes	These guys look fierce but are great friends.
Roadrunners, guineas, and other snake-eating birds	They control the dangerous snakes like rattlers, copperheads, coral, and water moccasins.
Most garden snakes are beneficial	Protect Nature's biodiversity.
Citronella	Spray as needed.
Cedar	Broadcast fine-textured material.

SQUIRRELS

Control	Application
Live traps	Use as needed.
Fox urine	Apply to problem areas. Works as a repellent.
Blood meal and/or cayenne or other hot pepper	Spread around problem area.
Truth?	Beats me how to control them!

TURTLES

Control	Application
Underwater traps for aquatic turtles	Use as needed.
Land turtles are mostly beneficial	Fence off vegetable garden.

NATURAL ORGANIC PRODUCTS

ORGANIC FERTILIZERS

Synthetic fertilizers hurt the soil and plants with every application. They are basically salts. One of the biggest problems with synthetic fertilizers is that they contain no organic matter and, therefore, no carbon. Soil microorganisms must have this carbon energy source, and, if it is not provided, the microbes will take it from the soil. That causes soil health reduction with every fertilizer application.

Organic fertilizers nourish and improve the soil. As opposed to synthetic fertilizers, they help the soil because they do not create high levels of salts such as nitrates, which disturb or even kill beneficial soil organisms. Organic fertilizers release nutrients slowly and naturally. All components in an organic fertilizer are usable by the plants, since there are no useless fillers as in synthetic fertilizers.

The nitrogen-phosphorus-potassium analysis (N-P-K) printed on bags of fertilizer by law is basically irrelevant in an organic program. Feeding the soil and plants with nothing but nitrogen, phosphorous, and potassium is like feeding your kids nothing but sodas. Soil and people need a balance of nutrients. For some unknown reason, fertilizer recommendations continue to emphasize these three nutrients with special

emphasis on high levels of nitrogen. A standard obsolete recommendation is a ratio of 3-1-2 or 4-1-2, such as 15-5-10 or 16-4-8.

Studies have shown that 80 percent or more of all synthetic nitrogen applied to the soil will be volatized or leached out, and the 20 percent or less that does reach the plant is harmful. Other studies show that an excess of chemical fertilizer slows or even stops the activity of microflora and microfauna such as beneficial bacteria, algae, fungi, and other microorganisms. Harsh fertilizers also cause damage to macroorganisms, such as earthworms, millipedes, centipedes, etc., which are extremely important to the natural processes in the soil.

High-nitrogen fertilizers also can cause severe thatch buildup in lawns by forcing unnatural flushes of green growth and retarding microbe activity. That's why mechanical thatch removal programs are often recommended for chemically maintained lawns. Organic lawn care programs take care of thatch problems naturally as the living microorganisms feed on the grass clippings and other dead organic material.

High-nitrogen fertilizers such as 15-5-10 (or even higher) are still being recommended by many in the farming, ranching and landscaping business. I've made the same recommendations myself in the past, but those amounts of nitrogen, phosphorous, and potassium are unnecessary and even damaging to soil health.

When healthy, the soil will produce and release nutrients during the decomposition process. The microbiotic activity releases tied up trace elements such as iron, zinc, boron, chlorine, copper, magnesium, molybdenum, and others, which are all important to a well-balanced soil.

The most important material in an organic program is organic matter, which becomes humus during the decomposition process. Humus becomes humic acid, other beneficial acids, and mineral nutrients.

Organic fertilizers are better than artificial products because they are the derivatives of plants and animals and therefore contain most or all the trace elements that exist in growing plants and animals. Synthetic fertilizers do not have this rounded balance of mineral nutrients.

In addition, organic fertilizers are naturally slow releasing and provide nutrients to plants when they need the nutrients. Synthetic fertilizers glut the plants with nutrients immediately after application, which is usually at the wrong time. The worst choices of all are the nitrogen only products such as ammonium sulfate (24-0-0).

ORGANIC FERTILIZERS AND SOIL AMENDMENTS

Alfalfa Meal: Alfalfa provides many nutritional benefits not only for plant use, but for soil organisms as well. One very important ingredient is tricontanol, a powerful plant growth regulator. Orchid and rose growers make alfalfa tea and spray it directly on as a foliar fertilizer. Alfalfa is very high in vitamins, plus N-P-K, Ca, Mg, and other valuable minerals. It also includes sugars, starches, proteins, fiber, and sixteen amino acids. Use at ten to twenty pounds per thousand square feet.

Alfalfa Tea: In a five-gallon bucket, put one cup alfalfa meal. Fill bucket with water and let it sit overnight. The result will be a thick tea. Apply generously to the root area of shrubs and flowers or use as a foliar spray after straining away the solids.

Bat Guano: A natural, all-purpose fertilizer containing nitrogen and lots of trace elements. The analysis will vary with the age of the guano. It has natural fungicidal qualities and has almost no chance of being contaminated with pesticides or chemicals. It is an excellent supplemental fertilizer for flowers. Best to apply once or twice during the growing season. It looks mild but has as much as 10 percent nitrogen, so be careful not to overuse.

Biosolids: The politically correct term for sewer sludge. An excellent organic fertilizer if not contaminated—which is possible since many toxins and heavy metals go down the drains. Fully composted products are the best and should be used primarily on roadways and other low use areas.

Blood Meal: Organic source of nitrogen and phosphorous. Good to use as a mix with cottonseed meal. Expensive but good to use occasionally. Analysis can range from 12-2 to 11-0-0. Does have a strong odor.

Bone Meal: Source of calcium and phosphorous recommended for bulbs, tomatoes, and other vegetables. Analysis will range from 2-12-0 to 4-12-0 with 2 to 5 percent calcium. Rock phosphate is better and cheaper.

Cattle Manure: Manure is one of our greatest natural resources. It has to be handled properly and not overused in any one area. Using too much of anything can cause problems. Manure can be properly used in several ways. Cow manure is a good ingredient for the manufacture of compost or for use directly on agricultural fields. Dairy cow manure is best because it has the least chance of chemical contamination. It should be composted prior to using in the home vegetable garden.

Cedar Flakes: Soil amendment good for chiggers, fleas, and lowering the pH of the soil. An effective material to use on the floor of greenhouses. Cedar flakes are an excellent control for harmful nematodes. Would be a staple organic product today if A&M hadn't sabotaged it.

Chelators: Chelated iron and other chelated nutrients are used when a direct dose of a particular nutrient is needed to quickly solve a deficiency. Chelated products are organic compounds with attached inorganic metal molecules, which are more available for plant use. Compost, humus, humic acid, and microorganisms have natural chelating properties.

Chicken Litter: Chicken litter is a good natural fertilizer high in nitrogen. Pelletized forms are better because they are not as dusty. Approximate analysis is 6-4-2. Unfortunately, commercial chickens are still being fed lots of unnatural things including arsenic. Best to compost before using. Nature's Creation is a Dirt Doctor endorsed product line that has been composted and spiked with beneficial fungi.

Coffee Grounds: Coffee grounds of any type make excellent fertilizer. They can be applied directly to the soil in beds or potted plants. Old coffee can also be used. Both are acidic and loaded with nutrients, including N-P-K.

Compost: The best fertilizer and the key to any organic program. Nature's own product, high in nutrients, humus, humic acid, and microorganisms. Compost has magical healing and growing powers and can be used successfully on any and all plants. Analysis will vary due to ingredients. Compost can be made at home or purchased commercially. The best composts are those made from a variety of organic material such as hay, sawdust, paunch manure, leaves, twigs, bark, wood chips, dead plants, food scraps, pecan hulls, grass clippings, and animal manure. The best manure to use is whatever is locally available: chicken, turkey, cattle, horse, rabbit, etc.

Corn Gluten Meal: Corn gluten meal is a natural weed and feed fertilizer. It should be broadcast in the spring before weed germination to prevent grassburs, crabgrass, and other annuals. For the cool season or winter weeds, broadcast again before germination in the fall fifteen to twenty pounds per thousand square feet for the control of henbit, dandelions, annual bluegrass, and other winter weeds. It also serves as a powerful organic fertilizer having about 9-10 percent nitrogen. Make sure the product you buy contains 60 percent protein. There are some inferior products on the market. The good stuff is available granulated and as a meal.

Cornmeal: A food product that, when used on the soil or in bed preparation, functions as a natural fungal disease control. Use it at ten to twenty pounds per thousand square feet to prevent or cure brown patch in St. Augustine, damping off disease, leaf spot diseases, etc. Grocery store cornmeal is not as effective as horticultural or whole-ground cornmeal. Organically ground cornmeal is the best, but much harder to find.

Cottonseed Meal: A good natural fertilizer with an acid pH. Analysis will vary and ranges from 6-2-1 to 7-2-2 with trace elements. Does have odor, but is a good organic source of nitrogen. As of this printing there is no good source of organically grown cottonseed meal.

Earthworm Castings: An effective organic fertilizer that is high in bacteria, calcium, iron, magnesium, and sulfur as well as N-P-K and has more than sixty trace minerals. Earthworm castings make an excellent ingredient in potting soil, in flats when germinating seed, and to toss into each hole when planting vegetables, herbs, or small ornamentals. It is a gentle, sweet smelling and clean organic fertilizer. Excellent for interior plants.

Fish Hydrolysate (or liquid fish): A concentrated liquid fish fertilizer for use directly in the soil or as a foliar feed. The analysis will range from 4-1-1 to 5-2-2. It is reported to be an effective insecticide. Good all-purpose spray when mixed with liquid kelp. Has an odor for about twenty-four hours—a pretty strong one, in fact. Fish emulsion is no longer recommended because of the processing method.

Fish Meal: A natural fertilizer originally used in this country by Native Americans growing corn. They used whole fish. Fish meal has a high analysis of approximately 8-12-2 but is also stinky, so use with caution. It is an excellent fertilizer for all plants, but is expensive.

Garrett Juice: Garrett Juice is a subtly powerful foliar feeding spray. It can be used as a liquid soil fertilizer as well. For foliar feeding, use the concentrate with water at two to three ounces per gallon and use on herbs, vegetables, groundcover, shrubs, vines, trees, turf grasses, and greenhouse plants. Garrett Juice is a blend of manure compost tea, seaweed, apple cider vinegar, and molasses. It can be used on any age plants, but it's always best to spray any liquid materials during the cooler parts of the day. For soil treatment, the application rate can be doubled. Garrett Juice provides major nutrients, trace minerals, and other beneficial components. See chapter 5 for recipe. Garrett Juice Plus contains fish hydrolysate and is manufactured by the Soil Mender Company.

Glauconite: (See greensand)

Granite Sand: Sand-like residue from the granite quarry or natural deposits. Excellent way to add minerals to planting beds. Much better than washed concrete sand. Contains potash and many trace minerals. Most sources also have paramagnetism.

Greensand: Material called glauconite, which is a naturally deposited undersea, iron-potassium silicate. It's an excellent source of iron and other trace minerals with a normal analysis of about 0-1-5. It's best used with other fertilizers and organic materials. Contains 14–20 percent iron.

Gypsum: This natural soil amendment material is calcium sulfate and is an excellent source of calcium and sulfur. Gypsum also neutralizes plant toxins, removes sodium from the soil, and opens the soil structure to promote aeration and drainage. Gypsum is approximately 23 percent calcium and 17 percent sulfate. It is usually not needed in high calcium soils.

Horse Manure: Horse manure is higher in nitrogen than most other farm animal manures and is an excellent material to use for the manufacture of compost. Fresh manures should not be tilled directly into the soil unless they are applied a month before planting or composted first. Sheep manure has similar properties and uses.

Humates: Leonardite shale is basically low-grade lignite coal and is an excellent source of carbon, humic acid, and trace minerals. Percentage of humic acid will vary. May be made into liquid form or used in the dry form.

Hydrogen Peroxide: An oxidizing liquid for use on soil in diluted amounts. A dangerous product in concentrated forms. It should be used at a 3 percent formulation to help aerate and flocculate the soil. Do not continue to use.

Kelp Meal: A dry fertilizer made from seaweed. Approximate analysis is 1-0-8 with many trace minerals and plant hormones that stimulate root growth and regulate plant growth. Seaweed also provides soil-conditioning substances, improves the crumb structure or tilth, and helps stimulate microorganisms.

Lava Sand: The sand-sized and smaller waste material left from lava gravel processing is an excellent, highly paramagnetic soil-amendment material. It can be used in potting soils and bed preparation for all landscaping and food crops. Finer textured material would be even better if it was easily available. Not needed in volcanic soils.

Lime: A major calcium fertilizer, dolomitic lime contains 30–35 percent magnesium. High-calcium lime is preferred because most low calcium soils have plenty of magnesium. High calcium lime is calcium carbonate.

Micronized Products — Such as those by Nature's Creation that have been mechanically processed into a powder. These products can be mixed with water and sprayed on foliage or drenched into the soil.

Mineral Products — Many on the market that contain rocks, including lava sand, basalt, granite sand, rock phosphate, humate, and montmorillonite. They are excellent soil amendments for most soils.

Mycorrhizal Products — Products such as those by Nature's Creation and others that contain living beneficial fungus that enhances root and plant growth.

Molasses: Sweet syrup that is a carbohydrate used as a soil amendment to feed and stimulate microorganisms. Contains sulfur, potash, and many trace minerals. Liquid molasses is used in sprays and dry molasses is used as an ingredient in organic fertilizers by itself.

Rabbit Manure: The average analysis of rabbit manure is around 2.5-1.5-5. Mixed with leaves, sawdust, straw, grass, and other vegetative materials, it makes an excellent compost. Can be used directly as a fertilizer without fear of burning plants. Llama and Opaca manures can also be used direct without composting first.

Rock Phosphate: Phosphate rock is formed in oceans in the form of calcium phosphate. Economic source of natural phosphorus and calcium. Used mainly for edible crops and flowering plants. It helps promote photosynthesis and helps deter weeds.

Root Stimulators: This is a generic term that refers to mild fertilizers or any material that stimulates microbial activity and root growth. Liquid seaweed, vinegar, molasses and compost tea also function as root stimulators. Most commercial root stimulators are simply liquid synthetic fertilizers and shouldn't be used. The foliar spray Garrett Juice also functions as a soil and root stimulator.

Seaweed: Best used as a foliar spray. Excellent source of trace minerals. Should be used often. Contains hormones that stimulate root growth and branching. Many trace elements are found in seaweed in the proportions they are found in garden plants. Seaweed contains hormones and functions as a mild, but effective, insect control—especially for whiteflies and spider mites. It acts as a chelating agent, making other fertilizers and nutrients more available to the plants. Seaweed or kelp is available in liquid and in dry meals.

Sul-Po-Mag: A naturally occurring mineral containing 22 percent sulfur, 22 percent potash, and 11.1 percent magnesium. An excellent specialty fertilizer product for the organic program.

Sulfur: A basic mineral often lacking in alkaline soils. Applying granulated sulfur at five pounds per thousand square feet twice annually can bring base saturation of calcium down and raise magnesium. Be careful not to breath dust, over-apply, or use when planting seed. It can act as a preemergent. Sulfur dust is also used as a pesticide in some situations. It should not be used in acid soils.

Turkey Manure: Turkey manure is a high-nitrogen product that is an excellent ingredient for compost making. It is too "hot" to use direct unless planting is delayed for several weeks.

> *The definition of a good organic product is this, "any material that when applied improves the balance and health of the soil."*

FERTILIZER CHART (GENERIC PRODUCTS)

Organic Fertilizers	N	P	K*	Comments
Alfalfa	3	1	2	Vitamin A, folic acid, trace minerals, and growth hormone "tricontanol."
Bat guano	10	3	1	High in nitrogen, phosphorus, and trace minerals.
Blood meal	12	1	1	Good nitrogen source but smelly.
Bone meal	2	12	0	Good calcium and phosphorus, calcium, and trace minerals.
Cow manure	2	1	1	Should be composted before use.
Colloidal phosphate	0	18	0	Excellent organic source of phosphorus, calcium, and trace minerals.
Compost	1	1	1	Best all-around organic fertilizer.

Corn gluten meal	9	1	1	60% protein, natural pre-emergent qualities
Cottonseed meal	7	2	2	Acid pH, lots of trace minerals.
Earthworm castings	1	.1	.1	Beneficial bacteria, trace minerals, humus, earthworm eggs.
Fish hydrolysate	5	2	2	Foliar plant food, helps with insect control. Some products have an odor.
Fish meal	7	13	3	Nitrogen, phosphorus, and lots of vitamins and minerals but smelly.
Granite sand	0	0	5	Low cost source of minerals, especially potash.
Greensand	0	2	5	Natural source of phosphorus, and lots of vitamins and minerals but smelly.
Horse manure	4	1	1	More powerful than cow manure.
Molasses	1	0	5	Food for microorganisms and source of sulfur and potash.
Rabbit manure	3	2	1	Not used enough, excellent source of natural nutrition.
Rock phosphate	0	18	0	Excellent source of phosphate.
Pig manure	1	1	.5	Good source of humus and microorganisms. Composted is best.
Poultry manure	5	3	2	High-nitrogen organic fertilizer, best to compost first.
Sheep manure	.5	.3	5	Good natural fertilizer.
Seaweed (dry)	1	0	1	Trace minerals and hormones that stimulate root growth and branching.
Seaweed (liquid)	1	0	1	Trace minerals and hormones that stimulate root growth and branching.
Sludge compost	5	3	0	Good product if not contaminated.
Sul-Po-Mag	0	0	22	Mined source of sulfur, potassium, and magnesium.
Tankage	6	8	0	Slaughter house by-product. Should not be used.

*The analysis of organic fertilizers will vary depending on the raw ingredients, processing, and age.

MANUFACTURED FERTILIZER OPTIONS

Organic Fertilizers	N	P	K	Comments
Bioform	4	2	4	Fish emulsion, seaweed, and molasses.
Bradfield	3	1	5	Alfalfa meal, molasses, potassium sulfate and poultry meal.
GreenSense	3	1	2	Composted manure, activated carbon, alfalfa, molasses, ferrous sulfate.
Garden-Ville	6	2	2	Compost, humate, bat guano, cottonseed meal.
Ladybug	8	2	4	Wide range of ingredients and university testing.
Maestro-Gro	6	2	4	Fish meal, bone meal, and other natural ingredients.
Medina Grow Green	4	2	3	Dry poultry manure, humate, molasses, and greensand.
Microlife	6	2	4	Organic products with a wide range of quality ingredients.
Nature's Creation	5	5	5	Micronized, composted poultry manure. Contains mycorrhizal fungi.
Nature's Guide	5	3	2	Poultry-based with molasses, seaweed, humate, and alfalfa.
Perfectly Natural	5	5	5	All-purpose with mix of corn gluten meal, organic animal and vegetable by-products, and other natural ingredients.
Soil Mender Yum Yum Mix	2	1	1	Mix of alfalfa, cottonseed, meal, greensand, humates, molasses, and several rock powders.
Sustane	5	2	4	Composted turkey manure.

FOLIAR FEEDING

Feeding the soil is the basis of organics. However, there are ways of stimulating the natural processes in the soil and in the plants without putting the material into the soil. Spraying the foliage of plants can provide some significant horticultural advantages.

Some foliar sprays such as hydrolyate (liquid fish), compost tea, humate, and seaweed are fertilizers. When fertilizer nutrients are sprayed directly on the foliage, immediate results can often be seen because the micronutrients, when taken in through the foliage, are immediately available to the plant.

When food crops or ornamentals have chlorosis (yellow leaves with green veins) resulting from lack of iron, magnesium, or other soil elements, spraying the foliage with natural products can create a greening improvement within a few days. Organic products have natural chelating abilities. Plants need green foliage to be able to produce food through the process of photosynthesis where sunlight, water, and carbon dioxide combine in the leaves to produce sugars and carbohydrates to feed the plant.

Some spray products are stimulators rather than feeders. They work by stimulating plant growth and flower/fruit production by increasing photosynthesis in the foliage, increasing the movement of fluids and energy within the plant, increasing root exudates and microbiotic activity in the soil at the root zone, and increasing the uptake of nutrients from the soil through the root hairs. In other words, foliar feeding can provide missing or "locked up" elements as well as stimulate all of the natural systems in the plant and in the soil. The end result is bigger, stronger, healthier plants with increased drought, insect, and disease resistance.

Here are some points to remember when using foliar sprays:

1. Less is usually better in foliar sprays. Light, regularly applied sprays are better than heavy, infrequent blasts. Mists of liquids are better than big drops, unless you are also trying to control pests.

2. High humidity increases a leaf's ability to absorb sprays. Spraying on damp mornings or evenings will increase the effectiveness of the spray. The small openings (stomata) on the leaves close up during the heat of the day so that moisture within the plant is preserved. The best time of day to spray is late afternoon for pest control. Daybreak is best for foliar feeding.

3. Young foliage seems to absorb nutrients better than old, hard foliage. Therefore, foliar feeding is most effective during the periods of new growth on plants.

4. Adding sugar or molasses in small amounts to your spray solutions can stimulate the growth of beneficial microorganisms on the leaf surfaces. The stimulation of friendly microbes helps to fight off insect pests and harmful pathogens.

5. Foliar feeding will increase the storage life of food crops. It will also increase cold and heat tolerance.

6. Don't use only foliar feeding. Soil feeding is also needed to keep the roots from getting lazy.

Foliar feeding has been used since 1844, when it was discovered that plant nutrients could be leached from leaves by rain. Experiments soon proved that nutrients could also enter the plant through the foliage. It's still somewhat of a mystery as to just exactly how the nutrients enter the plant through the foliage—but it is known and agreed that it works and works quickly. For something further to think about, there is also

Foliar feeding is an excellent way to give plants fertilizer elements that are lacking in the soil.

evidence that nutrients can be absorbed through the bark of trees. Spray away! Some of the best choices are Garrett Juice Plus, aerated compost, and Nature's Creation micronized products.

ORGANIC PEST CONTROL PRODUCTS

The following products and techniques are a guide for controlling insects with the least damage to nature's balances. The organic pesticides that kill insects are better choices than the toxic chemicals, but I hope you only use them as a last resort since most of the pesticides can't tell the difference between a good bug and a bad one.

Antidesiccants: Also called antitranspirants, these products are made from pine oil and are nontoxic and biodegradable. They are sometimes used for the prevention of powdery mildew on roses and crape myrtles. They work by spreading a clear film over the leaves. They are also used to help control diseases. I'm a little concerned about how they gum up the surface of the leaves.

Bacillus Thuringiensis **(Bt):** A beneficial bacteria applied as a spray to kill caterpillars. Sold under a variety of names such as Thuricide, Dipel, and Bio-Worm and others. Use *Bacillus thuringiensis* 'Israelensis' (Bti) in water for the control of mosquito larvae. Use Garrett Juice with Bt for extra effect. Spray at dusk and add one to two ounces of molasses per gallon spray. It provides protein and keeps insect-killing bacteria alive on the foliage longer—even during rain. Bt 'San Diego' is good for Colorado potato beetle, elm leaf beetle, and other leaf-chewing beetles.

Baking Soda: Mixed at the rate of four teaspoons per gallon (one rounded tablespoon), baking soda makes an excellent fungicide for black spot, powdery mildew, brown patch, and other fungal problems. Be careful to keep the spray on the foliage and not on the soil as much as possible. Baking soda is sodium and bicarbonate—both are necessary in the soil, but only in very small amounts. Potassium bicarbonate is a better choice for the same use at the same rate.

Black Hole Gopher Trap: Guaranteed to trap your gophers—so the ad says. Gophers are notoriously hard to get rid of—and annoyingly destructive. Even if they don't wolf down your entire harvest-to-be, their tunnels and mounds can ruin your garden. The black hole trap works only on gophers and is safe around pets and children. Gophers live in round tunnels and have learned that square things (like most traps) are dangerous, so this trap is round, like the tunnels. When the trap is placed at the end of its tunnel, the gopher detects the air and light that the trap lets in. When it rushes to plug it up, a snare catches and kills it.

Bordeaux Mix: A fungicide and insecticide usually made from copper sulfate and lime. I no longer recommend any products that use copper due to its toxicity.

Citrus Products: Orange, grapefruit, and other citrus peelings can be frozen and later ground up into a pulp to serve as an effective root knot nematode control. Mix the pulp into the soil at about two to five pounds per thousand square feet prior to planting crops that are susceptible to the pests. The same material can be used as a fire ant control by tossing it around the mounds for the ants to forage.

To make an excellent cleaner for counters, walls, bathroom fixtures, etc., mix one ounce of orange or other citrus oil into one quart of water. This mix can also be used to kill indoor insect pests, but is too strong to spray on plant foliage. Use at a rate of no more than two ounces per gallon of water as a pest control spray on plants. For outdoor use, it is best to mix with molasses and compost tea.

Copper: Trace mineral that in liquid form has been used as a fungal control. I no longer recommend it. It's too toxic and there are much better choices.

Diatomaceous Earth (DE): Natural diatomaceous earth is approximately 5 percent aluminum, 5 percent sodium, 86 percent silicon. It is the skeletal remains of microscopic organisms (one celled aquatic plants called diatoms) that lived in sea water or freshwater lakes millions of years ago in the western United States. Apply using a dusting machine and cover plants or treatment area entirely. Be sure to use a dust mask when applying! DE is non-selective, so use sparingly. Breathing any dusty material can cause lung problems. As a food supplement, use at 1–2 percent of the food volume for feeding pets or livestock. Swimming pool DE has been partially melted and is much more dangerous to breathe. Use only natural diatomaceous earth that contains less than 1 percent crystalline silica dioxide. The highest quality natural DE I have found is Soil Mender Diatomaceous Earth.

Never use swimming pool DE for anything other than pool filters.

Dormant Oil: Long-standing, winter treatment for scale and other over-wintering insects. Petroleum-based and will kill beneficial insects, so use sparingly. The correct name now is horticultural oil and it can be sprayed more than just in the winter. It works by smothering the over-wintering insects and is effective against scale, aphids, spider mites, and others. Do not use sulfur as a fungicide without waiting thirty days after using dormant oil.

Floating Row-Cover: Gardening fabric designed to envelope plants in a moist, greenhouse warmth while allowing water, light, and ventilation for proper plant respiration. Protects foliage from chewing insects, prevents flies and moths from laying eggs, and reduces diseases carried by pests. Birds, rabbits, and other animals are discouraged from feeding on plants. It is much better than plastic sheets and other materials.

Garlic-Pepper Tea: An organic insect and disease repellent material made from the juice of garlic and hot peppers such as jalapeno, habanero, or cayenne. This is one of the best preventative controls available. It is effective for both ornamental and food crops.

Hydrogen Peroxide: Spray at 3 percent formula for the control of most plant disease, including viruses.

Nicotine Sulfate: An old time, organic pesticide used for the control of hard-to-kill insects. Although it is a quickly biodegradable product, it is extremely dangerous to handle and I do not recommend its use.

Nosema Locustae: A biological control for crickets and grasshoppers. It works the same way *Bacillus thuringiensis* (Bt) works on caterpillars. It's applied as dry bait, the insects eat the material, get sick, and are cannibalized by their friends. Charming, isn't it? But it works. Brand names include Nolo Bait, Grasshopper Attack, Semispore and others.

Oils: There are now three types of spray oils: dormant, horticultural, and vegetable. Dormant oils are petroleum based, relatively free of impurities, and have been used as far back as 1880. Dormant oils have lower volatility and more insect-killing power than the other oils, but they can be more toxic to plants. These oils aren't recommended any longer. Horticultural oils are the lightest and most pure petroleum oils. They can be used for spraying pecan trees and fruit trees, but they are also effective on shrubs and flowers that have scale or other insect infestations. Vegetable oils are plant extracts. They are environmentally safe, degrade quickly by evaporation, fit into organic or integrated pest management programs, are nonpoisonous to the applicator, are noncorrosive to the spray equipment, and kill a wide range of insects. Many states are leaning toward vegetable oils. Drilling lubricants can no longer be petroleum oils.

Plant Wash: A fancy soap that is used to clean plants resulting in insect and especially disease control. It eliminates powdery mildew on crape myrtles, sooty mold on citrus, black spot on roses and many other plant diseases. Plants are vulnerable to ten thousand varieties of insects and eighty thousand diseases worldwide. Also an estimated 300,000 toxic pesticide poisonings occur in the U.S. every year. Plant ailments and diseases are easily prevented by hygiene, cleaning, and attention to problems. Plant Wash is an excellent cleaner of plants and most other things as well.

Pyrethrum: Available in liquid or dry forms. Will kill a wide range of insects including aphids, beetles, leafhoppers, worms, caterpillars, and ants. It is short-lived and mostly toxic to those applying the product. Pyrethrum is dried and powdered painted daisy *(Chrysanthemum cinerariae-folium)*. Artificial chemical substitutes, called pyrethroids, are even worse. Pyrethrin is the active ingredient in the natural product. Even though pyrethrum is a natural product, I strongly recommend not using it. There are less toxic alternatives that work better.

Rotenone: A botanical pesticide that was used to kill aphids, worms, beetles, borers, and thrips. No longer considered an acceptable organic product. Products available containing rotenone and pyrethrum are much too toxic. Safer alternatives exist that work as well or better. It is extremely dangerous to fish. Do not use.

Ryania: Root extract from the ryania shrub has been used as a dust or spray to control moths, corn borer, and other problem insects. Ryania is a relatively strong organic pesticide. I don't recommend it. Safer alternatives exist. Usually not available.

Sabadilla: A botanical insecticide made from a tropical lily. It is effective on some of the hard-to-kill garden pests such as thrips, cabbage worms, grasshoppers, loopers, leafhoppers, harlequin bugs, adult squash, and cucumber beetles. This is a toxic organic product that I no longer recommend—which doesn't matter since it isn't available anyway.

Soap: Nonphosphate liquid soaps and water mixed together into a spray are used to control aphids and other small insects. Strong solutions can damage plant foliage, even weak solutions can kill many of the microscopic beneficial insects and microorganisms—so use sparingly. The best of the soap products is Plant Wash.

Sulfur: Finely ground sulfur is used by mixing with water or dusting on dry plants to control black spot, leaf spot, brown canker, rust peach leaf curl, powdery mildew, apple scab, and many insect pests. Mix with liquid seaweed to enhance the fungicidal properties. Sulfur will also control fleas, mites, thrips, and chiggers. To avoid leaf burn, do not use when temperature is 90° or above. Sulfur will burn squash and other cucurbits such as pumpkins, gourds, and melons.

Tanglefoot: Spread on the bark of trees to control gypsy moths, canker worms, climbing cutworms, and ants. Made from natural gum resins, castor oil, and vegetable waxes. Old product that's useful in organic programs. Do not put all the way around plant trunks—it will girdle the plants. Apply in vertical strips or on a paper ring wrapped around the trunk first.

Vinegar: Vinegar has many horticultural uses. Natural apple cider vinegar is an ingredient in Garrett Juice, can be used as a mild fertilizer at one ounce per gallon of water. It is good for the dogs and cats at about one tablespoon per gallon of drinking water. Grain alcohol 10 percent vinegar is an important ingredient in the natural herbicide mixture. See appendix. 20 percent and higher vinegar is not recommended at all, nor is fake vinegar made from petroleum and sold as glacial acetic acid.

Weed Fabrics: Synthetic fabric that supposedly allows air and water movement, while at the same time blocking out some weed growth. Many people still recommend it under walkways, driveways, decks, and patios. I don't recommend. Use a thick layer of mulch instead in order to maintain the natural processes in the soil. The only place it seems logical to use is under gravel in utility areas.

Yellow Sticky Traps: Nontoxic, bright-yellow cards that trap insects with their sticky coating. They are primarily used to monitor insect populations. They give some effective control of white flies and other small insects in greenhouses.

COMPOST—MOTHER NATURE'S FERTILIZER

What is compost? How do you make a compost? Is compost a fertilizer? How do I use compost? Is composted manure in a bag really compost? Do I need bark, peat moss, and compost?

To answer all these questions, let's go through the entire composting process. For starters, everything on earth that's alive dies and everything that dies, rots—and completely rotted material is compost. Yes, compost is a fertilizer. In fact, it is the best fertilizer—being Nature's own. Compost is not only an excellent fertilizer, but also an excellent way to recycle waste. The word compost comes from two Latin words meaning "bring together."

The best composts are those that are made at home from several ingredients. The ideal mixture is about 80 percent vegetative matter and 20 percent animal waste. The best materials are those that you have on your own property. The second-best materials are those that can be easily gotten from near your property. The compost pile location can be in sun or shade, and covers are not necessary.

Even though there are many recipes for compost, it's almost impossible to foul up the compost-making process. For new gardens or planting beds, the composting can be done right on the ground by lightly tilling organic matter into the soil and mulching. To use this method effectively, it's best to do the work now and wait until next season to plant. Composting in the ground, as the forest does, simply takes longer than composting in a pile. Remember that composting is more of an art than a science and a little experimenting is good. There are many acceptable ways to build compost piles, but I find that the simplest systems are usually the best.

Compost—Mother Nature's Fertilizer

The best time to compost is whenever the raw materials are available. It's ideal to have compost piles working year round. Choose a convenient site—some easily accessible, utility area such as behind the garage or in the dog run. The most effective compost piles are made on a paved surface so that the liquid leachate can be caught and used as a fertilizer. When the pile is on the ground, the leachate is wasted but the earthworms can enter the pile and help complete the natural degradation of the material.

Next, decide what kind of a container to use. I don't use a container at all but instead just pile the material on the ground or on a concrete slab. If you choose to use a container, buy some hog wire, lumber, wooden pallets, cinder blocks, or any materials that will hold a volume of about four feet by four feet with a height of three feet. Compost piles should be at least three feet by three feet by three feet.

Hay or wheat-straw bales make an excellent container for compost. Build a two- or three-sided container by stacking the bales to make the sides. At the end of the composting process, the hay-bale sides can be pulled into the mix to become part of the compost. Wood containers will also rot and become part of the compost.

Everything that was once alive can and should be composted. Some include grass clippings, leaves of all kinds, sawdust, spent plants, weeds (don't worry about the weed seed), tree chips, coffee grounds, feather meal, seaweed, peanut hulls, pecan hulls, and other nut shells, fish scraps, brewery waste, slaughterhouse waste, paper, pine needles, wool, silk, cotton, granite dust, vegetable and meat scraps, fruit peelings and waste, pet hair, household dust, and animal manures. It's controversial whether dog and cat manure should be used in the compost pile. I don't have cats, but I do use the dog manure. You should make your own decision on this point. I usually do not recommend using newspaper or other dyed or printed materials, and never synthetic fabrics, burned charcoal, plastics or rubber.

The materials should be chopped into various-size pieces and thoroughly mixed together. Compost piles that contain nothing but one particle size will not breathe as well. Layering the ingredients, as most books recommend, is unnecessary unless it will help to get the proportions right. Remember that, after the first turning, the layers won't be there anymore. Also, remember that green plant material contains water and nitrogen and thus will break down faster than dry, withered materials. It's a good idea to add some native soil (a couple of shovels full) to each pile to inoculate the pile with native-soil microorganisms. To thrive, microorganisms need (1) an energy source, which is any carbon material such as dry leaves or wood (2) a nitrogen source such as manure, green foliage, or organic fertilizers (3) air and (4) moisture.

Watering the pile thoroughly is important and best done while mixing the original ingredients together. The proper moisture level is 40–50 percent, similar to the wetness of a squeezed-out sponge. Piles that are too wet will be anaerobic and not decay properly. Piles that are too dry won't compost properly or fast enough. Once you have gotten the pile evenly moist, it's easy to keep it there. Give it a little water during dry periods. If you have ants in your compost pile, it's too dry.

Turning the pile is important. Turning keeps the mixture aerobic by helping oxygen penetrate the material. Turning also ensures that all the ingredients are exposed to the beneficial fungi, bacteria, and other microorganisms that work to break the raw material down into humus. It also ensures that all the ingredients are exposed to the cleansing heat of the center of the pile. In a properly "cooking" compost pile, the heat of approximately 150° kills the weed seed and harmful pathogens, but stimulates the beneficial microorganisms. Don't be concerned if your pile heats for a while and then cools off—that's natural. The entire process takes anywhere from two months to a year depending on how often the pile is turned. If the ingredients contain a high percentage of wood chips, the process may take even longer. It's interesting that softwood sawdust and chips break down more slowly than hardwood.

Compost activators can be helpful in getting the pile to heat up and cook faster. Although most any organic fertilizer can be used as a compost activator, they should be mixed into the pile at three to four pounds per cubic yard of compost. Molasses can also help.

Compost can be used in many ways. Partially completed compost makes a very effective top-dressing mulch for ornamental or vegetable gardens. It's easy to tell when the compost is finished and ready to use as a fertilizer and soil amendment. The original material will no longer be identifiable, the texture will be soft and crumbly, and the fragrance will be rich and earthy.

Compost can be used to fertilize grass areas, planting beds, vegetable gardens, and potted plants. It is the best organic material for the preparation of new planting beds. Why is compost better than pine bark or peat moss? Because it's alive, it stimulates biological activity, is nutritious, recycles local and regional raw materials, and is much more cost effective.

What can be put in the compost pile?
Anything that was once alive.

APPENDIX

CONVERSION TABLES

CHEMICAL MIXING CHART AND RECIPES

Use this table to determine the amount of liquid/dry chemicals to add to water based on a standard of a given amount per 100 gallons in the manufacturer's instructions. Example: If the manufacturer recommends 8 oz. per 100 gallons, and 1 gallon of mix is required, read the table from left to right, 8 oz./100 gallon column over to ½ tsp./gallon column.

CHEMICAL MIXING CHART AND RECIPES

Liquid Equivalent Table

100 gal	25 gal	12½ gal	5 gal	1 gal
2 gal	2 qt	1 qt	12¾ oz	2½ oz.
1 gal	1 qt	1 pt	6½ oz	2½ tbs.
2 qts	1 pt	8 oz	3¼ oz	3¾ tsp.
3 pt	12 oz	6 oz	5 tbs.	1 tbs.
1 qt	½ pt	4 oz	3 tbs.	2 tsp.
1½ pt	6 oz	3 oz	2½ tbs.	1½ tsp.
1 pt	4 oz	2 oz	5 tsp.	1 tsp.
8 oz	2 oz	1 oz	3 tsp.	½ tsp.

Powder (Dry) Equivalent Table

100 gal	25 gal	12½ gal	5 gal	1 gal
5 lb	1¼ lb	12 oz	4 oz	4 ⅘ tsp.
4 lb	1 lb	8 oz	3½ oz	3 ⅘ tsp.
3 lb	12 oz	6 oz	2⅜ oz	2 ⅘ tsp
2 lb	8 oz	4 oz	1¾ oz	2 tsp
1 lb	4 oz	2 oz	⅞ oz	1 tsp
8 oz	2 oz	1 oz	⅜ oz	½ tsp.
4 oz	1 oz	½ oz	3/16 oz	¼ tsp.

1 oz. = 6 tsp. (liq.), 9 tsp. (dry); 1 oz. = 2 tbs. (liq.), 5 tbs. (dry); 1 tbs. = 3 tsp. (liq), 4 tsp. (dry)

APPLICATION RATE CHART

800 lbs./acre = 20 lbs./1,000 sq. ft.
400 lbs./acre = 10 lbs./1,000 sq. ft.
250 lbs./acre = 6 lbs./1,000 sq. ft.
200 lbs./acre = 5 lbs./1,000 sq. ft.
1 qt./acre = 2 tbs./1,000 sq. ft. = 1 oz./1,000 sq. ft.
13 oz./acre = 1 tsp./1,000 sq. ft. = 3 oz./1,000 sq. ft.
11 gal./acre = 1 qt./1,000 sq. ft.
1 qt./acre = 2 tbs./1,000 sq. ft.
1 lb./acre = .4 oz./1,000 sq. ft.
1.5 oz./acre = 7 drops/gal./1,000 sq. ft.
13 oz./acre = 1 tsp./1,000 sq. ft.
4 oz./acre = .10 oz./1,000 sq. ft. (30 drops per gal.)
8 oz./acre = .20 oz./1,000 sq. ft. (60 drops per gal.)
3.84 oz./gallon = 3% solution

Appendix

APPLICATION RATE CHART (continued)

1 gal./10 acres	=	13 oz./acre
1.5 gal./10 acres	=	19 oz./acre
.5 gal./10 acres	=	6 oz./acre
6" soil	=	2 million lbs./acre

1 ton/acre = 4.6 lb. per 100 sq. ft. = .4 lb. per sq. yd.
3 tons/acre = 14 lb. per 100 sq. ft. = 1.25 lb. per sq. yd.
10 tons/acre = 46 lb. per 100 sq. ft. = 4 lb. per sq. yd.
1 gal./10 acres = 13 oz./acre
1.5 gal./10 acres = 19 oz./acre
.5 gal./10 acres = 6 oz./acre
6" soil = 2 million lbs./acre

LINEAR MEASURE

1 foot	12 inches		
1 hand	$\frac{1}{3}$ foot	4 inches	
1 span	9 inches		
1 yard	3 feet		
1 rod	$16\frac{1}{2}$ feet	$5\frac{1}{2}$ yards	
1 furlong	40 poles	220 yards	
1 mile	8 furlongs	5,200 feet	320 rods
1 league	3 miles		
1 degree	$69\frac{1}{8}$ miles		

SQUARE OR AREA MEASURE

1 square foot	144 square inches	
1 square yard	9 square feet	
1 acre	160 square rods	43,560 sq. ft.
1 section	640 acres	1 square mile
1 hectare	2.47 acres	

COMMON MEASUREMENTS

One pinch/dash	$\frac{1}{16}$ tsp.
1 ounce	360 drops
1 teaspoon	$\frac{1}{6}$ ounce (60 drops)
1 tablespoon	3 tsp. ($\frac{1}{2}$ oz. liquid, 180 drops)
1 gallon (gal.)	769 tsp. (256 tbs., 128 oz., 16 cups, 8 pints, 4 qts.)
4 tablespoons	$\frac{1}{4}$ cup (2 ounces liquid)
$\frac{1}{3}$ cup	5 tablespoons plus 1 teaspoon
$\frac{1}{2}$ cup	8 tablespoons (4 ounces liquid)
1 gill	$\frac{1}{2}$ cup (4 ounces liquid)
1 cup	16 tablespoons (8 ounces liquid)
1 pint (pt.)	2 cups (16 ounces liquid)
1 quart (qt.)	2 pints (32 ounces liquid)
4 quarts	1 gallon
1 peck	8 quarts
1 bushel	4 pecks
1 pound	16 ounces (dry measure)
1 barrel (bbl.)	$31\frac{1}{2}$ gallons
1 acre foot	325,000 gallons

153

Appendix

CUBIC OR VOLUME MEASURE

1 cubic foot	1,728 cubic inches
1 cubic yard	27 cubic feet
2 cord of wood	128 cubic feet

(A legal cord of wood is 4 feet high, 4 feet wide, and 8 feet long.)

1 board foot   144 cubic inches $\frac{1}{12}$ cubic foot

METRIC EQUIVALENTS

Linear

1 millimeter (mm.)	.0394 in.	
1 centimeter (cm.)	.3937 in.	
1 decimeter (dm.)	3.937 in.	
1 meter (m.)	39.37 in.	1.1 yard
1 decameter	393.7 in.	10 yd. 2.8 ft.
1 hectometer	328 ft. 1 in.	
1 kilometer	3,280 ft. 1 in.	

CONVERSIONS

1 sq. yd.	9 sq. ft.
1 cu. yd.	27 cu. ft.

DRY MEASURE

1 quart	2 pints
1 peck	8 quarts
1 bushel (bu.)	4 pecks

COMMON EQUIVALENTS

1 bushel	2,150 cubic inches or 1 ¼ cubic ft.
1 gallon	231 cubic inches
1 cubic foot	7½ gallons
1 cubic foot of water	62½ pounds (62.43 lb.)
1 gallon of water	8⅓ pounds (8.345 lb.)
1 cubic foot of ice	57½ pounds

APPLICATIONS RATES (BULK MATERIAL)

(1 cu. ft.=)	(1 cu. yd.=)	(3 cu.ft. bagged)	(2 cu. ft. bagged)
12 sq. ft. 1" deep	1,296 sq. ft. ¼" deep	36 sq. ft. 1" deep	96 sq.ft. ¼" deep
6 sq. ft. 2" deep	648 sq. ft. 1/2" deep	18 sq. ft. 2" deep	48 sq.ft. ½" deep
4 sq. ft. 3" deep	324 sq. ft. l" deep	12 sq. ft. 3" deep	24 sq.ft. 1" deep
3 sq. ft. 4" deep	162 sq. ft. 2" deep	9 sq. ft. 4" deep	12 sq.ft. 2" deep
	108 sq. ft. 3" deep		8 sq.ft. 3" deep
	81 sq. ft. 4" deep		6 sq.ft. 4" deep

CONVERSION TABLES

U.S.		Abbreviations		Metric	
1 teaspoon	60 drops	Teaspoon	t.	1 teaspoon	5 milliliters
1 tablespoon	3 teaspoons	Tablespoon	T.	1 tablespoon	15 milliliters
1 tablespoon	180 drops	Cup	c.	1 ounce	30 milliliters
1 ounce	2 tablespoons	Pint	pt.	1 quart	.940 liters
1 ounce	360 drops	Quart	qt.	1 gallon	3.76 liters
1 cup	8 ounces	Gallon	gal.		
1 pound	16 ounces	Ounce	oz.		
1 pint (I6 oz.)	2 cups	Pound	lb.		
1 quart (32 oz.)	2 pints	Milliliter	ml.		
1 gallon (128oz.)	4 quarts	Liter	l.		
1 gallon	16 cups				
1 gallon	128 ounces				

DILUTION CHART (Gallons of Water)

Dilution	1 Qt.	1 Gal.	3 Gal.	5 Gal.	10 Gal.	15 Gal.
1–10	3 oz.	12 oz.	2¼ pts.	2 qts.	3¾ qts.	5½ qts.
1–50	4 t.	5 T.	7½ oz.	12½ oz.	25 oz.	37½ oz.
1–80	1 T.	2 oz.	6 oz.	10 oz.	20 oz.	30 oz.
1–100	2 t.	2½ T.	3½ oz.	6¼ oz.	12½ oz.	19 oz.
1–200	1 t.	4 t.	2 oz.	3½ oz.	6½ oz.	10 oz.
1–400	½ t.	2 t.	2 T.	1½ oz.	3 oz.	5 oz.
1–800	—	1 t.	1 T.	5 t.	1½ oz.	2½ oz.

SOIL NUTRIENT AVAILABILITY

Nutrient	Low	Normal	High	Very High
Calcium	<20 percent	20–60	60–80	>80
Magnesium	<10 percent	10–25	25–35	>35
Potassium	<5 percent	5–20	20–30	>30
Phosphorus	<.1 percent	.1–.4	.5–.8	>.8
Nitrogen	<1 ppm	1–10	10–20	>20
Nitrate	<5 ppm	5–50	50–100	>100
Sulfate	<30 ppm	30–90	90–180	>180
Sulfur	<10 ppm	10–30	30–60	>60

ppm represents parts per million
Percentage represents available percentages in the soil.

PRODUCT RATE CHART

Product	Rate	Frequency/Comments
Alfalfa meal	20 to 25 lbs./1,000 sq. ft.	Once a year in conjunction with other organic fertilizers.
Bat guano	10 to 20 lbs./1,000 sq. ft.	Once a year to flowering plants or at each flower rotation.
Blood meal	10 to 20 lbs./1,000 sq. ft.	May be combined with cottonseed meal (4 parts cottonseed meal to 1 part blood meal).
Bone meal	80 to 100 lbs./1,000 sq. ft.	Once a year when planting bulbs or flowers. Watch for calcium buildup.
Cow manure	20 to 30 lbs./1,000 sq. ft. up to 5 tons/acre	Use composted manure to avoid weeds; raw material good to use on agricultural fields. Watch for buildup of phosphates and nitrates.
Cottonseed meal	20 to 30 lbs./1,000 sq. ft.	Use once or twice a year. May be combined with blood meal or other meals.
Rock phosphate	25 to 50 lbs./1,000 sq. ft.	Use once/year to give a long-lasting source of phosphorus and calcium. Put small handful into planting hole of new plants.
Compost	¼-inch depth on lawns; 2-inch depth in beds. 900–1,200 lbs./ac. on agriculture fields	Once a year to lawns and planting beds is ideal. Not important if beds are mulched.
Earthworm castings	10 lbs./1,000 sq. ft.	Use once/year or at each annual flower rotation on flowering plants as a supplemental food. Put a small handful in each planting hole.
Epsom salts	1 tbs./gal.	Spray monthly if needed. Can be mixed with other sprays. For soils deficient in sulfur and magnesium.
Fish hydrolysate	2 oz./gal of water/1,000 sq. ft.	Spray all plants 2 to 3 times/year or any time extra greening or pest control is needed.
Fish meal	20 lbs./1,000 sq. ft.	Once or twice a year to lawns or planting beds as a supplemental fertilizer. Use 10 pounds/1,000 sq. ft. after the first year.

Product Rate Chart, Continued

Product	Rate	Frequency/Comments
Granite sand	10 lbs./1,000 sq. ft. up to 5 tons/acre.	Once a year as a mineral supplement. Can also be used to top-dress new, solid-sod installations.
Greensand	10 to 20 lbs./1,000 sq. ft.	Excellent mineral supplement.
Humate (Dry)	5–10 lbs./1,000 sq. ft.	Use high quality humate (40–50 percent, humic acid) at 50 lbs./acre once/year.
Humate (Liquid)	1–2 oz./1,000 sq. ft.	Spray all foliage lightly 3 times/ growing season. Can be mixed with other liquid products.
Hydrogen peroxide (H_2O_2)	1 oz of 35 percent material per gal./1,000 sq. ft. or 8 oz. of 3% material/gal./1,000 sq. ft.	Can be mixed with other materials but always add the H_2O_2 first.
Lava sand	10 lbs./1,000 sq. ft. up to 5 tons/acre	Once a year as a mineral supplement. Can also be used to topdress new solid sod installations.
Manure on fields	500–1,000 lbs./acre	In the beginning, as much as 5 tons/acre can be used until fertility levels increase.
Minerals Plus	20–40 lbs./1,000 sq. ft.	Apply as needed to add trace minerals and to increase soil paramagnetism.
Molasses	1 oz./gal. of water or other liquids dry-20 lbs./1,000 sq. ft.	Apply as a foliar and soil spray to fertilize and feed microbes.
Molasses (dry)	5–10 lbs./1,000 sq. ft.	Apply to soil that is not yet healthy. One application a year is usually enough.
Organic fertilizers in general	20 lbs./1,000 sq. ft.	½ tsp./4" pot, 1 tsp./gal, 1 tbs./5 gal. container. Water in after application.
Poultry manure	20 lbs./1,000 sq. ft. the first year; 10 pounds thereafter. Composted only	Apply twice/year as a good natural source of nitrogen.
Seaweed (Liquid kelp)	½ to 1 oz./1,000 sq. ft.	Apply to lawns and planting beds once a month as a supplement between applications of dry fertilizers.

Appendix

Product Rate Chart, Continued

Product	Rate	Frequency/Comments
Seaweed (Kelp meal)	10 to 20 lbs./l,000 sq. ft.	Apply to lawns and planting beds once a month as a supplement between applications of dry fertilizers.
Seaweed and Fish emulsion	Mix 1 oz. of seaweed and 2 oz. of fish emulsion/gallon of water	Apply as a general foliar spray to aid insect and fungus control and as a foliar feed. Spray all plants and lawns.
Soybean meal	20 lbs./1,000 sq. ft.	Apply twice/year.
Sul-Po-Mag	20 lbs./1,000 sq. ft.	Use once/year on soil needing sulfur, magnesium, and potassium.
Vinegar	½ oz./gal.	Mix with other liquid products use 1 to 2 gal. of mix/1,000 sq. ft.

DILUTIONS

How to dilute is a constant question to the Dirt Doctor.

How do I convert 20 percent vinegar to 10 percent vinegar?
In Simple terms:

You want to reduce the strength of the vinegar by 1/2 (from 20 percent to 10 percent).

Remove 1/2 of the total contents from your container and set aside. Then replace with water the amount that you removed from container, which will give you 10 percent Vinegar Solution. Do the same for the portion of vinegar you set aside. You will now have 2 containers of 10 percent vinegar. I do not recommend 20 percent vinegar. Too strong!

How do I make 30 percent vinegar to 10 percent?
In Simple terms:

You want to reduce the strength of the vinegar by 2/3 (from 30 percent to 10 percent).

Divide the vinegar from your container into 3 equal amounts. Return one part (1/3) of the amount back into the original container Replace with water the amount you removed from original container. Do the same with the two remaining 1/3 parts vinegar you set aside. You will now have 3 containers of 10 percent vinegar. However, vinegar this strong (30 percent) should never be bought or used.

HOMEMADE FORMULAS

ANT CONTROL (INTERIOR): Crushed or chopped pieces of tansy leaf or bay leaf will repel ants quite effectively. A light dusting of cinnamon is also very effective.

For ant baits, use the following:

1 teaspoon of creamy peanut butter
1 pat of butter or oleo
1 tablespoon of any light syrup
1 teaspoon of boric acid powder

Blend the above ingredients over low heat until smooth—be careful not to burn the solution. Put the finished bait into lids or other small containers. The ants will find them. This amount will make several bait stations—feed ants as long as they will take the bait. Do not use this recipe on your waffles or pancakes. Remember that boric acid is poison. Change the sweet ingredients from time to time to prevent the ants from catching on.

BAKING SODA FUNGICIDE: Mix 4 teaspoons (about 1 rounded tablespoon) of baking soda and 1 teaspoon of liquid soap or vegetable oil into one gallon of water. Spray lightly on foliage of plants afflicted with black spot, powdery mildew, brown patch, and other fungal diseases. Avoid overusing, and try to keep out of the soil. Do not mix baking soda with other sprays. Potassium bicarbonate is even better than baking soda and is used in the same way.

COMPOST TEA: Compost tea is effective on many pests because of certain microorganisms that exist in it naturally and because of others that it stimulates perennials, annuals, vegetables, roses and other plants. It's effective on black spots on roses and early blight on tomatoes. How to dilute the dark compost tea before using depends on the compost used. A rule of thumb is to dilute the leachate down to one part compost liquid to four to ten parts water. It should look like iced tea. Be sure to strain the solids out with old pantyhose, cheese cloth or row cover material. Malcolm Beck says fill the container full compost, slowly add water and use anytime after 36 hours. See compost tea making instructions on page 64.

CORNMEAL TEA: Cornmeal Juice is a natural fungal control for use in any kind of sprayer. Make by soaking horticultural or whole ground cornmeal in water at one cup per gallon of water and then straining out the solids. Put the cornmeal in a nylon stocking bag to hold in the larger particles. The milky juice of the cornmeal will permeate the water and this mix should be sprayed without further dilution. Cornmeal Juice can be mixed with compost tea, Garrett Juice or any other natural foliar feeding spray. It can also be used as a soil drench for the control of soil borne diseases.

FIRE ANT MOUND DRENCH: Equal parts compost tea or liquid humate, molasses, and orange oil. Mix 4-6 ounces per gallon of water to drench fire ant mounds. Use only 2-4 ounces per gallon for spraying plants for insect pests.

FLY REPELLENT: Hang clear plastic bags filled with water. It really works.

GARLIC FLY KILLER: Recycle the pulp from the garlic tea preparation by adding some water to solids and set it outside—several feet from the back door. It not only attracts flies but *kills* them in the process. Later toss it in the compost pile.

GARLIC-PEPPER TEA INSECTICIDE: Liquefy 2 bulbs of garlic and 2 hot peppers in a blender 1/3 full of water. Strain the solids and add enough water to the garlic/pepper juice to make 1 gallon of concentrate. Use ¼ cup of concentrate per gallon of spray. For added strength, add 2 ounces of citrus oil for each gallon of water in the sprayer. To make garlic tea, omit the pepper and add another bulb of garlic.

GARRETT JUICE: You can buy Garrett Juice commercially or you can make your own. Per gallon of water add 1 cup manure compost tea concentrate, 1 ounce molasses, 1 ounce apple cider vinegar, 1 ounce liquid seaweed. For added disease control: ¼ cup garlic tea. For added fertilizer power add liquid fish. The commercial product that contains fish is Garret Juice Plus from Soil Mender.

ORGANIC HERBICIDE:

    1 gallon full strength 10 percent vinegar
    1 ounce orange oil
    1 tablespoon molasses
    1 teaspoon Plant Wash

ORANGE OIL PESTICIDE: For spraying insects on plants add 2 ounces of orange oil or d-limonene per gallon of water. Add 1 ounce of liquid molasses for more buffering. For indoor pests (not on plants) add 1 ounce of orange oil per quart of water.

REPELLENT FOR PETS, RABBITS, AND SQUIRRELS
Dog-B-Gone—1 part cayenne pepper, 1 part dry mustard powder, 2 parts flour. Sprinkle on top of ground. Don't water in! Rover will quit

going there eventually and mark other territory, and you will no longer need to treat original area. Will need to re-treat if there is rain. Cayenne pepper by itself usually works. Habanero works even better. Nothing works very well on squirrels.

ROACH BAITS: A non-toxic bait can be made by mixing Arm and Hammer detergent together in a 50-50 mix with sugar. To make boric balls, mix 1 teaspoon boric acid, 1 cup flour, ½ cup sugar, and water. Roll into cakes and place behind appliances out of the reach of pets and children.

Note: Remember, DE (diatomaceous earth) for pets and pests is not the same as swimming pool DE. Buy DE only from your local organic retailer.

TREE GOOP: 1/3 of each of the following mix in water: soft rock phosphate, natural diatomaceous earth, manure compost. Slop it on the trunk. Note: fireplace ashes can be substituted for the soft rock phosphate.

Note: Keep all insecticides away from children and pets. Don't breathe the dust of any dusty products. And remember that anything chemical or organic can injure or can kill if mishandled—there is no such thing as nontoxic.

Note: Never store homemade brews in glass or any tightly sealed container.

PUBLICATION RESOURCES

Agriculture Testament and *Soil Health* by Sir Alfred Howard are state-of-the-art guides to organics and the use of compost to bring soil back to health. They were written in the 1940s, but are still two of the best publications on the market. Oxford and Rodale Press.

The Albrecht Papers by William Albrecht is a compilation of papers by the late Dr. Albrecht and is considered the bible for managing soil health. Acres U.S.A.

Stones by Julius Hensel is a classic explaining the role of earth minerals in the production of wholesome food crops. Acres U.S.A.

Common Sense Pest Control by William Olkowski, Sheila Daar, Helga Olkowski is an excellent reference for low-toxicity pest control. The Taunton Press.

Dirt Doctor's DIRT is a monthly magazine sent to members of the Dirt Doctor's Ground Crew. For information to join call 1-866-444-DIRT or go to *DirtDoctor.com*

Growing Great Garlic, Ron Engeland, Acres USA, 800-355-5313.

Herbs for Texas by Howard Garrett covers the landscape, culinary, and medicinal uses of Texas native and introduced herbs. Odena Brannam helped with this book. University of Texas Press in Austin, Texas.

Howard Garrett's Texas Organic Gardening provides organic information specifically for Texas, including plant varieties, planting instructions, and maintenance techniques. Houston: Gulf Publishing Company, 1993.

How to Have a Green Thumb Without an Aching Back, Exposition Press, *Gardening Without Work,* Devin-Adair, and *The No Work Gardening Book,* Rodale Press, by Ruth Stout are great. She was a humorous writer, a philosopher, and an advocate of mulching.

Landscape Design...Texas Style by Howard Garrett. This book is a well-kept secret about my design and landscape philosophy as well as a rather decent reference book on landscape construction and regional plant material selection. Out of print but can be found in libraries.

Mother Nature's Herbal by Judy Griffin, Ph.D. Llewellyn Publications, St. Paul, MN.

Nature's Silent Music by Dr. Phil Callahan explains how to preserve the health of the land by avoiding toxic chemicals and working within nature's laws and systems. Acres U.S.A.

The One-Straw Revolution by Masanobu Fukuoka is an introduction to natural farming and an excellent book on the philosophy and practicality of organic gardening from one of Japan's living legends.

Organic Method Primer Basics by Bargyla Rateaver not only explains how plants absorb chunks of materials, including whole bacteria, they have electron microscope photos of the process in action. Books are available from Acres USA.

Seaweed and Plant Growth by Dr. T.L. Senn explains in detail the wonderful powers of seaweed as a fertilizer, growth stimulator, and pest repellent.

The Secret Life of Compost by Malcolm Beck is a "how to" and "why" guide to composting. Acres U.S.A.

Silent Spring by Rachel Carson is a must-read. If you don't convert to organics after reading this classic, you never will. The Riverside Press, Cambridge.

The Stockman Grass Farmer is a monthly publication of Allan Nation covering sustainable organic and holistic land management and livestock management. 1-800-748-9808.

Texas Bug Book by Howard Garrett and Malcolm Beck is a complete review of the beneficial and pest insects of Texas. University of Texas Press.

ORGANIC ROSE PROGRAM

Roses should only be grown organically since they are one of the best medicinal and culinary herbs in the world. When they are loaded with toxic pesticides and other chemicals, that use is gone, or at least, it should be. Drinking rose hip tea or using rose petals in teas or salads sprayed with synthetic poisons is a really bad idea. For best results with roses, here's the program:

Selection: Buy and plant well adapted roses such as antiques, David Austins and proven hybrids. The old roses will have the largest and most vitamin C filled hips. Rosa rugosa roses have the most vitamin C.

Planting: Prepare beds by mixing the following into existing soil to form a raised bed: 6" compost, ½" lava sand, ½" expanded shale, ½" of decomposed granite, 30 lbs. of wheat/corn/molasses soil amendment and 20 lbs. of sul-po-mag per 1,000 sq. ft. Soak the bare roots or rootball in water with one tablespoon of Garrett Juice per gallon. Settle the soil around plants with water - no tamping.

Mulching: After planting, cover all the soil in the beds with one inch of compost or earthworm castings followed by 2-3" of shredded native tree trimmings. Do not pile the mulch up on the stems of the roses.

Watering: If possible, save and use rainwater. If not, add one tablespoon of apple cider vinegar and one oz. Garrett Juice per gallon of water. If all that fails, just use tap water, but don't over water. Avoid using salty well water if possible.

Feeding Schedule:

Round #1 **February 1-15:** Organic fertilizer @ 20 lbs. per 1,000 sq. ft., lava sand @ 80 lbs. per 1,000 sq. ft. and horticultural cornmeal at 10 -20 lbs. per 1,000 sq. ft.

Round #2 **June 1-15:** Organic fertilizer @ 20 lbs. per 1,000 sq. ft, greensand @ 40 lbs. per 1,000 sq. ft. or soft rock phosphate at 30 lbs. per 1,000 sq. ft. if in acid soil areas.

***Round #3* September 15-30:** Organic fertilizer @ 20 lbs. per 1,000 sq. ft., sul-po-mag @ 20 lbs. per 1,000 sq. ft. Apply wheat/corn/molasses soil amendment at 30lbs. per 1,000 sq. ft.

PEST CONTROL
For disease control in general, spray roses with garlic tea or mild vinegar. For insect pests, spray plant oil products. For black spot, powdering mildew and other diseases, spray with Plant Wash. For thrips, apply beneficial nematodes to the soil in early spring.

ORGANIC PECAN AND FRUIT TREE PROGRAM
Pecan trees and fruit trees can be grown organically, and you don't have to spray toxic pesticides. Pecans should never have bare soil. The root zone should always be covered with mulches and/or native grasses and legumes.

SOIL FEEDING SCHEDULE

***Round #1* February 1-15:** Organic fertilizer @ 20 lbs. per 1,000 sq. ft. Lava sand or other volcanic sand at 80lbs. per 1,000 sq. ft., decomposed granite at 80 lbs. per 1,000 sq. ft. and horticultural cornmeal at 20 lbs. per 1,000 sq. ft.

***Round #2* June 1-15:** Organic fertilizer @ 10 lbs. per 1,000 sq. ft and Texas greensand @ 40-80 lbs. per 1,000 sq. ft. or soft rock phosphate at the same rate if in acid soils.

***Round #3* September 15-30:** Organic fertilizer @ 10 lbs. per 1,000 sq. ft. and sul-po-mag @ 20 lbs. per 1,000 sq. ft.

Notes: Once soil health has been achieved, round #3 can be omitted. Rock powders are optional after the first 3 Years.

Large pecan orchards can use livestock manure or compost at 1-2 tons/acre per year along with establishing green manure cover crops. Lava sand and other rock powders can be applied any time of the year. Foliar feed with Garrett Juice monthly.

FRUIT AND NUT SPRAY PROGRAM

Spray Garrett Juice at least monthly. Add garlic tea and/or Plant Wash if pest insects appear.

Spray Schedule

1st spraying: At pink bud. Use additional sprayings as time and budget allow.

2nd spraying: After flowers have fallen. For best results spray every two weeks, but at least once a month.

3rd spraying: About June 15th.

4th spraying: Last week in August.

Pruning

Very little pruning is needed or recommended. Maintain cover crops and/or natural mulch under the trees year round. Never cultivate the soil under pecan and fruit trees.

Insect Release

Trichogramma wasps: Weekly releases of 10,000 - 20,000 eggs per acre or residential lot starting at bud break for 3 weeks.

Green lacewings: Release at 4,000 eggs per acre or residential lot weekly for one month.

Ladybugs: Release 1,500 - 2,000 adult beetles per 1,000 sq. ft. at the first sign of shiny honeydew on foliage.

EDIBLE & MEDICINAL LANDSCAPING PLANTS

(These are all herbs - not 'erbs)

SHADE TREES:
- **Ginkgo** - tea from leaves
- **Jujube** - fruit
- **Linden** - tea from flowers
- **Mulberry** - fruit
- **Pecan** - edible nuts
- **Persimmon** - fruit
- **Walnut** - edible nuts

SHRUBS:

Agarita - fruit for wine
Althea - edible flowers
Bay - tea and, food seasoning from leaves
Germander - freshens air indoors
Pomegranate - edible fruit
Turk's cap - flowers and fruit for tea

ANNUALS:

Begonias - edible flowers
Daylilies - edible flowers
Dianthus - edible flowers
Ginger - food, seasoning and tea from roots
Hibiscus - edible flowers
Johnny jump-ups - edible flowers
Nasturtium - edible leaves
Pansies - edible flowers
Peanuts - edible nuts
Purslane - edible leaves
Sunflower - edible seeds and flower petals

VINES:

Beans and Peas - edible pods and seed
Gourds - dippers and bird houses
Grapes - food (fruit and leaves)
Luffa - sponges from the fruit, edible flowers
Malabar spinach - edible foliage
Passion flower - edible fruit, tea from leaves

ORNAMENTAL TREES:

Apple - fruit and edible flower petals
Apricot - fruit and edible flower petals
Citrus - edible fruit
Crabapple - fruit and edible flower petals
Fig - fruit and edible flower petals
Mexican plum - fruit
Peach - fruit and edible flower petals
Pear - fruit and edible flower petals
Persimmon - fruit
Plum - fruit and edible flower petals
Redbud - edible flowers
Rusty blackhaw viburnum - edible berries
Witchhazel - tea from leaves

PERENNIALS:

    Anise hyssop- edible flowers, foliage for tea
    Blackberries - edible berries, foliage for tea
    Chives - edible foliage and flowers
    Garlic - edible flowers, greens and cloves
    Hibiscus - edible flowers
    Hoja santa - leaves for cooking with meats
    Horsemint - insect repellent
    Jerusalem artichoke - roots for food
    Lavender - teas and insect repellent
    Monarda - edible flowers and leaves for teas
    Peppers - edible fruit
    Purple coneflower - all plant parts for teas
    Rosemary - food and tea from leaves and flowers
    Roses - petals and hips for tea
    Salvia - edible flowers, foliage for teas
    Sweet marigold - food, flavoring and tea from leaves and flowers
    Tansy - chopped and crushed foliage repels ants
    Turk's cap - flowers & fruit for tea

GROUND COVERS:

    Clover - tea from leaves and flowers
    Creeping thyme - teas and food flavoring
    Gotu kola - tea from leaves
    Mints - food and teas from flowers and leaves
    Oregano - teas and food flavoring
    Violets - leaves in salads and tea from flowers and leaves

Note: Pregnant women should avoid all strong herbs and no plant should be ingested in excess by anyone. None of these should be eaten unless they are being grown organically.

FLOWER CHOICES

Eating flowers has been done throughout the world for centuries. Roses and orange flowers are commonly used in Middle Eastern and Persian foods; lilies are used in China; cherry blossoms and chrysanthemums are used in Japan; lavender is a favorite in England and France; and the Mediterranean countries enjoy saffron in their food. Of course not all flowers are edible—some are poisonous either naturally or from toxic chemical pesticides. Only eat flowers grown organically. Flowers from florists, nurseries and traditional garden centers should not be eaten. If your garden center is organic, eat away.

8 RULES FOR EDIBLE FLOWERS

1. Not all flowers are edible. Some are poisonous. Learn the difference.

2. Eat flowers only when you are positive they are edible and nontoxic.

3. Eat only flowers that have been grown organically.

4. Do not eat flowers from florists, nurseries or garden centers unless you know they've been maintained organically.

5. Do not eat flowers if you have hay fever, asthma or allergies.

6. Do not eat flowers growing on the side of the road.

7. Remove pistils and stamens from flowers before eating. Eat only the petals of the larger flowers.

8. Introduce flowers into your diet the way you would new foods to a baby—one at a time in small quantities.

Note: Pregnant women should avoid all strong herbs and no plant should be ingested in excess by anyone at anytime. None of these plants should be eaten unless they have been grown organically. Edible flowers can be used to enhance food at breakfast, lunch and dinner. They can also be used in teas. Here are some of the best edible flower choices.

FLOWER CHOICES
Aloe vera, althea, apple blossoms, arugula, basil, begonia, borage, broccoli, calendula, chicory, chives - onion and garlic, clover, coriander, dandelion, dill, elderberry, English daisy, fennel, hyssop lavender, lemon, lilac, mint, monarda - red flowered M. didyma, mum (base of petal is bitter), mustard, okra, orange, oregano, pea (except for sweet peas), pineapple sage, radish, redbud, rosemary, scented geranium, society garlic, sweet woodruff, squash blossoms, thyme, violet, winter savory, yucca (petals only)

SICK TREE TREATMENT

Trees succumb to insect pests and diseases because they are in stress and sick. Mother Nature then sends in the clean up crews. Insects and pathogens are just doing their job - trying to take out the unfit plants. Most plant sickness is environmental - too much water, not enough water, too much fertilizer, wrong kind of fertilizer, toxic chemical pesticides, compaction of soil, grade changes, ill-adapted plant varieties and/or over planting single plant species and creating monocultures, as was done with American elms in the Northwest and the red oak/live oak communities in certain parts of the South.

My plan is simple. Keep trees in a healthy condition so their immune systems can resist insect pests and diseases. It has been noticed by many farmers and ranchers that oak wilt doesn't bother some trees - especially those that are mulched and those where the natural habitat under trees has been maintained. The Sick Tree Treatment is not just good for oak wilt, but for any other tree disease as well. Here is how it works.

Sick Tree Treatment
Step 1: Remove Excess Soil from above the Root Ball
A very high percentage of trees are too deep in their containers and also have been planted too low or have had fill soil or eroded soil added on top of the root flares. Soil on top of the root flare reduces oxygen availability and leads to circling and girdling roots. Soil, or even heavy mulch, on trunks keeps the bark constantly moist which can rot or girdle trees. Excess soil and circling and girdling roots should be removed before planting. Removing soil from the root flares of already planted trees should be done professionally with a tool called the Air Spade. Homeowners can do the work by hand with a stiff broom or gentle water and a shop-vac if done very carefully. Vines and ground covers should also be kept off tree trunks.

Step 2: Aerate the Root Zone Heavily
Don't rip, till or plow the soil. That destroys all the feeder roots. Punch holes (with turning forks, core aerators or agriculture devices such as the Air-Way) heavily throughout the root zone. Start between the drip line and the trunk and go far out beyond the drip line, 6-8" deep holes are ideal, but any depth is beneficial. An alternative is to spray the root zone with a living organism product such as Nature's Creation with mycorrhizal fungi.

Step 3: Apply Organic Amendments
Apply greensand at about 40-80 lbs. per 1,000 sq. ft., lava sand at about 80-120 lbs. per 1,000 sq. ft., horticultural cornmeal at about 20-30 lbs. per 1,000 sq. ft. and dry molasses at about 10-20 lbs. per 1,000 sq. ft. Cornmeal is a natural disease fighter and molasses is a carbohydrate source to feed the microbes in the soil. Expanded shale applied at 1/2 " is also very helpful if the budget allows this step. Apply a 1" layer of compost followed by a 3" layer of shredded native tree trimmings; however, do not pile mulch up on the root flare or the trunk. Smaller amounts of these materials can be used where budget restrictions exist.

Step 4: Spray Trees and Soil

Spray the ground, trunks, limbs, twigs and foliage of trees with compost tea or the entire Garrett Juice mixture. Do this monthly or more often if possible. For large-scale farms and ranches, a one-time spraying is beneficial if the budget doesn't allow ongoing sprays. Adding garlic oil tea or cornmeal juice to the spray is also beneficial for disease control while the tree is in trouble. Cornmeal Juice is a natural fungal control that is made by soaking horticultural or whole ground cornmeal in water at 1 cup per 5 gallons of water. Screen out the solids and spray without further dilution. Cornmeal Juice can be mixed with compost tea, Garrett Juice or any other natural foliar feeding spray. It can also be used as a soil drench for the control of soil borne diseases. Dry granulated garlic can also be used on the soil in the root zone at about 1-2 lbs. per 1000 sq. ft. for additional disease control. Adding PLANT WASH to the spray is also beneficial.

Step 5: Stop Using High Nitrogen Fertilizers and Toxic Chemical Pesticides

Toxic chemical pesticides kill beneficial nematodes, other helpful microbes and good insects, and also control the pest insects poorly. Synthetic fertilizers are unbalanced, harsh, high in salt, often contaminated and destructive to the chemistry, the structure and the life in the soil. They also feed plants poorly.

P.S. During drought conditions, adding soil moisture is a critical component.

TREE GOOP

1/3 of each of the following mixed in water:

rock phosphate
natural diatomaceous earth
manure compost

Slop it on the trunk.
Note: fireplace ashes can be substituted
for the rock phosphate.

GLOSSARY

ACID SOIL: Soils with a pH less than 7. If the pH is near 6, a soil is considered slightly or moderately acid; if below 5.5, it is very acid.

AERATION: A mechanical process of punching holes or ripping the soil, used to relieve the effects of soil compaction.

AEROBIC: An environment containing oxygen. In the soil, aerobic conditions favor organisms that oxidize organic residues and produce carbon dioxide as a major byproduct.

AGRISPON: A mineral and plant extract product that stimulates microorganisms and basic soil and plant functions. Manufactured in Texas by Appropriate Technologies.

ALKALINE SOIL: Soil with a pH greater than 7.

AMMONIUM NITRATE: 33-0-0 (NH4-NO3) A water soluble chemical compound containing approximately 33.5 percent nitrogen, one half of which is the ammonia form and one half in the nitrate form. Should not be used.

AMMONIUM PHOSPHATE: A solid fertilizer material manufactured by reacting ammonia with phosphoric acid. Should not be used.

AMMONIUM SULFATE: 21-0-0 (NH4)2SO4) A solid material manufactured by reacting ammonia with sulfuric acid. Should not be used.

ANAEROBIC: Without oxygen. Anaerobic decomposition is less efficient than aerobic organisms. Nitrogen fixation by free-living organisms usually occurs under anaerobic conditions.

ANHYDROUS AMMONIA: 82-0-0 (NH3) A gas containing approximately 82 percent nitrogen. Under pressure, ammonia gas is changed to a liquid and usually is stored and transported in this form. Anhydrous ammonia is used to make most of the solid forms of nitrogenous fertilizers and also is used for direct application to the soil either as a gas or in the form of aqua ammonia. The most soil-destructive fertilizer in the world.

ANION: An ion with a negative electrical charge. Sulfur, phosphorous, boron, chlorine, and molybdenum exist in the soil as anions.

ANION EXCHANGE: A condition, analogous to cation exchange, where one anion can replace another at the surface of a clay mineral.

ANTIDESICCANTS: Liquid sprays used to coat the foliage of plants for the purpose of reducing transpiration in hot weather and increasing cold tolerance in winter.

BACILLUS THURINGIENSIS (Bt): Biological insecticides that specifically target caterpillars and other problem insects.

BANDING FERTILIZER: The process of spreading fertilizer in bands rather than broadcasting it. The fertilize may be spread along a line about two inches to the side of a planted seed and sometimes two inches below. It is considered one of the best methods for utilizing commercial soluble fertilizers, especially phosphorus.

BAT GUANO: Bat poop.

BIODIVERSITY: Biodiversity of life is not just important, it's critical. The outstanding characteristics of nature are variety and dynamic stability. A healthy situation exists when we create ranches, farms, gardens, and landscapes that have a complex mix of microorganisms, insects, animals, and plants. To understand nature is to grasp the concept that nature is a whole and can't be subdivided. Everything relates to everything else.

BLOOD MEAL: A dry, organic fertilizer made of the blood from slaughterhouses. Normal analysis will be approximately 12-0-0.

BONE MEAL: Cooked bones ground to a meal without any of the gelatin or glue removed. Steamed bone meal has been steamed under pressure to dissolve and remove part of the gelatin.

BORAX: A salt (sodium borate) used in fertilizer as a source of the minor plant-food element boron. Borax contains about 11 percent of the element boron. It is available in food stores and is a suitable fertilizer for supplying boron. Use only in very small amounts. Best to avoid.

BORDEAUX MIX: A fungicide and insecticide made by mixing solutions of copper sulfate and lime, or of copper arsenate and phenols. Use the first one.

BUFFER CAPACITY: The degree to which a substance can resist changes in its characteristics.

BURNED LIME: Limestone heated to drive out carbon dioxide. Same as quicklime.

CALCAREOUS: Containing a high percentage calcium or calcian carbonate.

CALCITE: Limestone containing mostly calcium carbonate, $CaCO3$. A more common name is ground agricultural limestone.

CALCIUM CARBONATE: The principal component of calcitic limestone and one of the principal components of dolomitic limestone, of which magnesium carbonate, $MgCO_3$ is the other Marl and oyster shells also are composed primarily of calcium carbonate.

CARBOHYDRATES: Stabilized structures of sugars. Carbohydrates form the skeleton of the plant, and they are a means for storing energy for a long period of time.

CATION EXCHANGE: A process in which the small number of cations dissolved in the soil water (soluble cations) change place with the much larger number of cations associated with the soil micelles (exchangeable cations).

CATION EXCHANGE CAPACITY: A measure of the ability of the soil components to attract cations and hold them in exchangeable form. The exchange capacity depends upon the amount of clay, the type of clay, the organic content, and the degree of humification of the organic matter.

CEC: An abbreviation for cation exchange capacity.

CYTOKININ: A plant hormone that can modify plant development by stimulating or altering the cellular RNA.

CHELATION: The chemical process by which an organic substance binds a cation having more than one electrical charge. Chelation is similar to cation exchange. Cation exchange holds the majority of the major cation nutrients (calcium, magnesium, potassium), while chelation holds the cation trace elements (copper, iron, manganese, zinc).

CLIPPINGS: Leaves cut off by mowing.

C/N RATION: An abbreviation for carbon/nitrogen ratio.

COLLOIDAL: A state of matter where finely divided particles of one substance are suspended in another.

COLLOIDAL PHOSPHATE: Waste material from rock-phosphate mining operation. An excellent, slow-release source of phosphorous, calcium, and trace elements.

COMPACTION: The pressing together of soil particles by foot or vehicular traffic.

COMPANION PLANTING: Using different plants together that assist one another with insect and disease control.

COMPOST: Nature's fertilizer created by the rotting of vegetable and animal matter.

COMPOSTED MANURE: Animal manure that has been taken through the process of natural composting in order to kill pathogens and weed seed.

COOL-SEASON TURFGRASS: Those turfgrasses primarily used in the northern United States, such as Kentucky bluegrass, tall fescue, and ryegrass.

COPPERAS: Ferrous (iron) sulfate used as a trace nutrient fertilizer, especially in alkaline soils.

COPPER SULFATE: Most common source of copper for fertilizer. Also used as an insecticide and fungicide. A common name is blue vitriol. Toxic product that should not be used.

COTTONSEED MEAL: Fertilizer meal made from ground cottonseed.

COVER CROP: A crop that improves the soil on which it is grown. Many plants are sown primarily as cover crops to cover the ground, improve it, and protect it for a seeding cash crop. Other plants, such as alfalfa, clover, and most grass-legume sods, can serve as both a cash crop and a cover crop.

CROSS-POLLINATE: To apply pollen of a male flower to the stigma or female part of another flower.

CURCULIO, PLUM: Worm that attacks the fruit of plums and other orchard trees.

CUTTING HEIGHT: The distance between the ground and the blades of the mower.

DAMPING OFF: A disease of seeds and young seedlings caused by fungi.

DENITRIFICATION: The conversion of nitrates in the soil to some form of gaseous nitrogen, which escapes into the atmosphere and is lost.

DICOTYLEDON (DICOT): A plant with two seed leaves.

DIOECIOUS: Plants that have the male reproductive system on one plant and the female on another.

DORMANT TURF: A brown-colored turf that has temporarily ceased growth due to unfavorable environmental conditions.

ECO-EXCEMPT: An acceptable plant oil product for insect control.

EPIPHYTIC: Referring to plants growing without soil and receiving their nutrients from the air.

EXCHANGEABLE CATIONS: Those cations that are electrostatically attracted to soil particles. The sum of the exchangeable cations and the soluble cations is considered to constitute the available cations for plant take-up.

FERTIGATION: The application of fertilizer through an irrigation system.

FERTILIZER: Any material or mixture used to supply one or more soil or plant nutrients.

FISH EMULSION: An oily liquid fertilizer made from fish waste or whole fish. There are chemicals involved in the process.

FISH HYDROLYSATE: Fish fertilizer made from whole fish.

FLOWERS OF SULFUR: Finely granulated sulfur dust, used to acidify an alkaline soil.

FOLIAR BURN: An injury to the leaves of the plant, caused by the application of a fertilizer or pesticide.

FOLIAR SPRAY: Liquid plant nutrients applied by spraying on the foliage.

FOOTPRINTING: Discolored areas, or impressions, left in the lawn from foot traffic when the turf is in the first stage of wilt.

FRENCH DRAIN: A drainage device in which a hole or drench is backfilled with sand or gravel.

FUNGICIDE: A product used to control diseases caused by fungi.

GEOTROPISM: The effect of gravity on plants.

GREEN MANURE: A cover crop used to smother weeds, to protect the soil, and to hold nutrients that might otherwise be leached. Traditionally a green manure is planted after the harvest of a cash crop, but an alternative is a "living mulch," where a cover crop is sown before harvesting the cash crop.

GUANO: Decomposed dried excrement of birds and bats and is used for fertilizer purposes. The most commonly known guano comes from islands off the coast of Peru and is derived from the excrement of sea fowl. It is high in nitrogen and phosphate, and at one time was a major fertilizer in this country.

HAY: Grass, clover or the like that is cut while still green and used as a fodder or mulch.

HERBICIDE: A product used for weed control.

HUMUS: The Latin word for soil or earth. It is the broken-down form of organic matter.

HYDROMULCHING: A method of seeding using a mixture of seed, fertilizer and mulch, sprayed in a solution on the soil surface.

HYDROSEEDING: Same as hydromulching but without the mulch.

HYDROSPRIGGING: Same as hydromulching but uses sprigs instead of seed.

ION: An electrostatically charged atom formed when a salt is dissolved in water. The dissolved salt breaks up into both positively and negatively charged ions.

IONIC CHARGE: The electrical charge associated with ions. Cations have a positive electrical charge and anions a negative charge.

INSECTICIDE: A product used to control insects.

INTEGRATED PEST MANAGEMENT: Buzz word for using a little bit of organics and a varying bit of chemicals.

IRRIGATION, AUTOMATIC: An irrigation system using preset timing devices.

LANGBEINITE: Sul-Po-Mag.

LAYERING, SOIL: An undesirable stratification of a soil.

LEACHING: The movement (usually loss) of dissolved nutrients as water percolates through the soil.

LEATHER TANKAGE: Waste from the leather tanning industry. Not for use in an organic program.

LIME: Technically, lime is calcium oxide. In agricultural usage, however, the term is used to denote any liming material.

LIQUID FISH: Another name for fish hydrolysate.

LIME SULFUR: Organic pesticide used for disease control.

LOCALIZED DRY SPOT: An area of soil that resists wetting.

MAGNESIA: Magnesium oxide, used as an emergency source of magnesium.

MAGNESIUM SULFATE: A soluble salt used as a source of magnesium. Common forms are the mineral kieserite and Epsom salts.

MANALFA: Organic fertilizer made from a blend of livestock manure and alfalfa.

MANGANESE SULFATE: A solid chemical compound used as a source of manganese for plants.

MANURE: Manure most commonly refers to animal dung, but the term is also used in association with green manuring.

MINERAL OIL: Oil made from reined petroleum products.

MOLYBDENUM: One of the essential micronutrients.

MONOECIOUS: Plants that have male and female flowers on the same plant.

MYCORRHIZAL FUNGI: Fungi which penetrates roots of plants to extract carbohydrates. Its unique value is that in return it passes mineral nutrients to the plant. It can be a major source of available phosphorus. It is similar to the rhizobia bacterial that inhabit legume roots and fix nitrogen.

NECTAR: A sweet liquid secreted by plants. The main raw material of honey.

NEMATODES: Small hair-like organisms that attack root systems and other soil borne organisms.

NITRATE INHIBITORS: Substances that retard the ability of soil organisms to transform ammonium to nitrates. Their purpose is to avoid the denitrification which occurs with heavy fertilizer applications of urea, ammonium salts, or liquid ammonia.

NITRATE OF SODA: Sodium nitrate ($NaNO_3$) A fertilizer material containing approximately 16 percent nitrogen. The principal source of sodium nitrate has been the natural deposits of the salt in Chile. It is also produced synthetically. Do not use.

NITRIFICATION: A process which takes place in the soil thereby soil microorganisms form nitrates from organic matter and the ammonia forms of nitrogen.

NPK: A shorthand notation for "Nitrogen-Phosphate-Potash."

OPEN POLLINATED: Unlike hybrids, plants that will return true from seed.

ORGANIC MATTER: Organic substances in differing stages of decay, varying from litter to very stable humus.

OVERSEEDING: Seeding a dormant turf with a cool-season grass in order to provide color during the winter.

PEAT: A low-quality humus in which the nitrogen is completely lost through anaerobic fermentation. An anti-microbial product that should be replaced with compost.

PESTICIDE: A chemical used to control any turfgrass pest, such as weeds, insects, and diseases.

pH: An abbreviation for potential hydrogen, used chemically to express the hydrogen ion concentration of a solution. More simply, pH is a scale from 1 to 14, used to denote the relative intensity of acidity or alkalinity. A neutral solution, or soil, has a pH of 7.0. Values below 7.0 denote more acid conditions, and those above 7.0 more alkaline conditions.

PHOSPHATE: The fertilizer oxide form of phosphorus (P_2O_5).

PHOSPHORIC ACID: 0-52-0 to 0-55-0 (H_3PO_4) An inorganic acid used in the manufacture of concentrated calcium phosphates and ammonium phosphates and sometimes for direct application through irrigation water.

PHYTOPHTHORA: Botanical Latin name for a genus of fungi that causes plant disease, generally a root and crown-rot pathogen.

PHOTOSYNTHESIS: Nature's process of manufacturing carbohydrates from carbon dioxide (CO_2) and water (H_2O) with the use of light energy and green plant pigment called chlorophyll.

PLANT METABOLISM: Those functions of a plant that use energy stored in sugars and carbohydrates to enable the plant to grow and reproduce.

PLUGGING: Establishing a turfgrass using plugs of sod.

POLLEN: A mass of microspores in a seed plant. Looks like a fine dust.

POLYSACCHARIDES: Carbohydrates (complex sugars) of high molecular weight including starch and cellulose.

POTASH: A term used to denote potassium oxide (K_2O) equivalent of materials containing potassium.

POTASSIUM CHLORIDE: 0-60-0 (KCI) Muriate of potash.

POTASSIUM MAGNESIUM SULFATE: ($2mGso_4k_2so_4$) Also called Sul-Po-Mag and langbeinite. From natural salt deposits primarily in New Mexico and some European countries. Organic source of K, Mg, and S.

POTASSIUM SULFATE: (K_2SO_4) A solid material with a K_2O equivalent of 45 to 52 percent. Also called sulfate of potash.

PROTEINS: The active, amino acid components of growing plants. Proteins carry out the bodily activities of the plant, using the energy from sugars and carbohydrates.

PYRETHRUM: Natural insecticide made from the powder of the crushed painted daisy, *Chrysanthemum cinerariaefolium*. Very toxic and not recommended.

QUICKLIME: Burned lime, roasted to drive out carbon dioxide and increase the solubility.

REEL MOWER: A mower that cuts grass by means of a reel guiding the leaves against the cutting edge of the bed knife.

RENOVATION: Improving the vigor of a low-quality soil.

RHIZOBIA: A group of bacteria that penetrates the roots of legumes, extracting carbohydrates from the plant, and capable of fixing atmospheric nitrogen.

RHIZOME: A below-ground stem capable of producing a new plant.

RHIZOSPHERE: The soil area immediately adjacent to the root hairs of plants.

ROCK POWDERS: Naturally occurring materials with fertilizing value. The most common rock powders are limestone, rock phosphate, granite dust, greensand, langbeinite (sulfate of potash magnesia), and basalt.

ROOT NODULES: Nodules attached to the roots of legumes and certain nonlegumes. These nodules contain nitrogen fixing bacteria or nematodes.

ROTARY MOWER: A mower that cuts grass with a high-speed blade that runs parallel to the soil surface.

SALT INDEX: The relation of solubilities of chemical compounds. Most nitrogen and potash compounds have a high index, and phosphate compounds have a low index. When applied too close to seed or on foliage, the ones with high indexes can cause plants to wilt or die.

SCALD: Grass that dies under "standing water."

SCALPING: The excessive removal of leaves during mowing, leaving mostly stems.

SECONDARY ELEMENTS: The secondary plant food elements as traditionally defined are calcium, magnesium, and sulfur.

SLAG: A byproduct of steel, containing lime, phosphate, and small amounts of other plant food elements such as sulfur, manganese, and iron.

SOAP: A cleansing and emulsifying agent made by action of alkali on fat or fatty acids.

SOD: Plugs, squares, or strips of turf still connected to soil.

SOIL: An ecological system consisting of inorganic minerals, organic matter, and living organisms.

SOIL pH: The pH of the water in soil. It controls the availability of phosphorus and trace elements and the diversity of soil organisms. The soil pH for most soils is in the range 5.0 to 9.0, with 7.0 being neutral.

SOIL STRUCTURE: The distribution and size of aggregates in the soil. A good soil structure contains aggregates of widely varying size.

SPREADER SETTINGS: Most broadcast spreaders, set fully open, will dispense this fertilizer at approximately 10 pounds per 1,000 square feet per pass.

SPRIGGING: Establishing a lawn using sprigs or stolons.

STOLON: An above-ground stem capable of growing a new plant.

STRAW: The above-ground vegetative growth of a plant, usually a small grain or annual legume.

SUGAR: The direct product of photosynthesis. Sugars store the energy absorbed from the sun in the plant leaves.

SUPERPHOSPHATE: The first manufactured phosphorus fertilizer, prepared originally by dissolving bones in sulfuric acid. 0-18-0 to 0-20-0. Good product, but hard to obtain.

SUPERPHOSPHORIC ACID: 0-67-0 to 0-76-0. Not acceptable for use.

TANKAGE: Process tankage is made from leather scrap, wool, and other inert nitrogenous materials by steaming under pressure with or without addition of acid. This treatment increases the availability of the nitrogen to plants. Not acceptable for use in an organic program.

THATCH: A layer of organic matter that develops between the soil and the base of the plant.

TOPDRESSING: Spreading a thin layer of soil on the lawn to smooth the surface.

TRANSITION ZONE: An east-west zone through the middle of the US between the northern area, growing cold-season turfgrasses, and the southern area, growing warm-season turfgrasses.

TRIPLE SUPERPHOSPHATE: Rock phosphate dissolved in phosphoric acid. Hugely problematic and not recommended.

UREA: 45-0-0 - A solid synthetic organic material containing approximately 45 percent nitrogen. The only synthetic fertilizer that contains carbon. Is used in some "bridge" or "transitional" products.

UREA-FORM: Synthetic fertilizer (38-0-0).

VERTICAL MOWING: The use of mechanical devices that have vertically rotating blades for thatch control.

VOLATILIZATION: The process of liquid becoming a gas.

WARM-SEASON TURFGRASS: Those turfgrasses used primarily in the southern United States, such as Bermuda grass, St. Augustine grass, zoysia grass, centipedegrass, and buffalo grass.

WILT: The discoloration and folding of leaves caused by either excessively dry or excessively wet conditions.

INDEX

A

actinomycetes, 7-9,17

aerating, 13,21,59,64,123

aeration, 8,21,45,57,62,65,136

Albrecht, William A., 4,50,161

alfalfa, 13,34,47,50,52,68,93,114,
133,138,140,156

alfalfa meal, 133

alfalfa tea, 133

algae, 7,9,13,17,132

allergies, 126

aloe vera, 106

ammonium sulfate, 132

animals, 3-4,7,10,17,20,23,26,
63-64,91-92,102-104,110,
132,145

ant control, 159

anthracnose, 118,120

antitranspirants, 143

ants, 67,110

aphid lions, 94

aphids, 33,57,69-70,73,75,81,83,
87,89,92-94,96,99,110,120,
122,145-146

application rate chart, 152-153

armadillos, 127

armyworms, 110

B

Bacillus thuringiensis (Bt), 70,75,77,
79,81,83,99,101-103,106,
110-111,113-117,143,145

Bacillus thuringiensis 'Israelensis'
(Bti), 106,113,143

Bacillus thuringiensis 'San Diego' (Bt),
111,143

bacteria, 7-10,17,19,60,64,71,
118,132,135,139,143,150,162

bacterial blight, 118,120

Bactimos briquettes, 106

bagworms, 77,79,99,110

baits, 99,110,114,128,159

baking soda, 15,99,143,159

baking soda fungicide, 159

balm, 115,126

bark, 23-24,38-39,43-44,47-48,
50-52,64,69,79,85,119,134,
143,147-148,150,169

basil, 28,31,33,70,78,168

bat guano, 68,133,140

bats, 113,127,140

Beck, Malcolm, 25,91-92,122,159,
162-163

beds, preparation of, 43-45

bee balm, 126

bees, 41,29-30,100,110,126

beetles, 11,33,57,77,79,92-93,95,
97,100,102,104,110-111,143,
146,165

Bermuda grass, 52,125

bicarbonate, 120-122

Bio-Blast, 109

spider mites, 108,116

spiders, 11,57,96,116

spurge, 128

square or area measure, 153

squash bugs, 33,108,115

squash vine borers, 108,115

squirrels, 129,160-161

St. Augustine decline, 120

St. Augustine grass, 119-120,125

stimulators, 114

stink bugs, 108,115

straw, 68,84,123,137,149

sugar, 13,15,17,20,110,114, 133,141,161

sulfate, 23,140,145,155

sulfur, 12,14,18-19,44,56,75,79, 101,103,111,119,135-139,145, 147,155-156,158

Sul-Po-Mag, 14,83,138-139,158, 163-164

Sustane, 140

sweet marigold, 28,32

T

Tahoka daisy, 36

take-all-patch, 122

tanglefoot, 95,147

tankage, 139

tansy, 32,33,103,110-111,159,167

termites, 10-11,97,116

Texas Bug Book, 92,97,163

Texas greensand, 72,76,164

Texas Organic Vegetable Gardening Book (Garrett and Beck), 27

The Missing Link, 63

thrips, 70,73,93-94,109,116, 146-147,164

thuricide, 143

thyme, 28,32-33,70,78,167-168

ticks, 33,73,75,77,79,103,109, 111,116-117

tilth, 3,16,44,46-47,136

Tim-Bor, 109

tobacco horn worm, 116

tomato pin worm, 117

traps, 104,111,114-115,117, 127-129,143,147

Tree (Trunk) Goop, 110,114, 161,170

tree trimmings, 21,24-26,34, 41,45,47,52,56,64,75,79,85,87, 89,114,163,169

treehoppers, 117

trees, 5,21,25,27-28,38-42, 48-50,52-57,61,66-72,74,76, 78,80-84,86,88-89,93,96, 99-102,105-108,110,114, 118-119,125,127,135,143,145, 147,164-165,169-170

trichogramma wasps, 21,70,73,75, 77,79,81,83,96,101,103,110, 115-117

tricontanol, 47,133,138

trimmings, 52,114

turkey manure, 138

turtles, 115,129

U

urine, 128-129

V

vegetables, 7,15,23,28,30,32-34, 45-47,50-52,66,68,72,74,76, 78,80,82,85-87,92,102-103, 109,120,124,129,133,135,140, 145,147,149-150,159

verbena, 70,74,76,78

Complimentary Six Month Membership in the Dirt Doctor's Ground Crew

Join the Ground Crew to learn how easy and cost effective organic gardening and living is! It's informative, it's educational and organic gardening and living has never been so fun!

Organic Forums – Discuss organics and hundreds of related topics and share your thoughts with other people who care passionately about natural, organic gardening and living.

The Dirt Doctor Video Network – Videos on subjects that will teach how to live the Natural Way. You can watch the videos over and over again, whenever it is convenient for you.

The *DIRT* – An online magazine with great articles, helpful information, garden calendar, pictures, links and the best features to be found on natural organics.

For more information visit: www.DirtDoctor.com or call **866-444-3478 (DIRT)**

Send the completed form to: Dirt Doctor's Ground Crew
Free 6 Month Membership
P.O. Box 140650
Dallas, TX 75214

Name_____

Address_____

City _____State _____ Zip _____

Phone:_____

Email Address: _____

Please choose a forum name (user name) and password to activate your membership.

*Forum name (user name)_____

*Password_____

*(*User name and password are case sensitive)*

No reproductions. Original form only.